POCKET PRAYERS
ROBERT C.
SAVAGE

W🌐rld Wide
A ministry of the Billy Graham Association

1303 Hennepin Avenue
Minneapolis, Minnesota 55403

This special edition is printed with permission
from the original publisher, Tyndale House
Publishers, Inc., Wheaton, Illinois 60187

Third printing, November 1982

Library of Congress Catalog Card Number 82-60017
ISBN 0-8423-4849-2
Copyright © 1982 by Robert C. Savage
Printed in the United States of America

Nestled in the
wooded sand dunes,
with an awe-inspiring view
of Lake Michigan,
is the Prayer Tower
of the Maranatha
Bible Conference.

It is a most
appropriate memorial chapel
in memory of
Henry H. Savage—my dad.
Each morning
during the conference season
many climb to this historic,
"close-to-God" spot
and experience the joy
of intercession and praise.

To these
PRAYER TOWER PEOPLE
I dedicate this book.

CONTENTS

Introduction: How to Pray for Others   9
Matthew   13
Stomachs and Fenders   19
Luke   21
Earthquakes   31
John   33
What Is Your Number One Request?   37
Acts   39
A Bushel of Hershey Bars   45
Romans   47
Should We Kneel?   53
1 Corinthians   55
Three Ways God Answers   63
Galatians   65
Long or Short Prayers?   69
Ephesians   71
Turn on the Praise Faucet!   77
Philippians   79
Pray While Driving   83
Colossians   85
Pray Without Ceasing   89
1 Thessalonians   91
Arrows from the Quiver of Prayer   93

1 Timothy   95
More Arrows   99
2 Timothy   101
The Lines Are All Busy!   105
Titus   107
We Are Lazy   109
Hebrews   111
But I Can't Pray in Public   115
James   117
Two Questions   119
1 Peter   121
Quotable Quotes   125
2 Peter   127
Definitions of Prayer   129
1 John   131
I Wish I Had Your Corn   135
Jude   137
You Be the Compiler!   139
Psalms   141
Verse Index   156

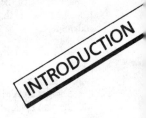

How to Pray for Others

Dear God, bless our pastor and all the missionaries.
Bless everybody, everywhere. Amen.

That's one way to pray, but it is neither sensible,
nor very rewarding. In fact, that kind of praying soon
becomes dull and boring.

The plan suggested in this book can make your
prayer life . . . exciting . . . meaningful . . . biblical
. . . enjoyable.

Instead of repeating the same words over and over
in praying for the various ones you wish to remember,
try this approach. In this book are over 700 Bible-based
requests you can use as you intercede for those
the Lord has placed upon your heart.

You've probably never heard of Henry Woolnough,
but I'll never forget him. He came to Quito, Ecuador,
when he was in his seventies, to live with his missionary
daughter on the compound of Radio Station HCJB
(The Voice of the Andes). The outstanding thing about
him was his prayer life. He had a list of more than
700 missionaries he prayed for every day. Those of us
who were on his prayer list were indeed fortunate.

I often wondered what Brother Woolnough said to the
Lord about each one on his list. Perhaps the requests
in this book would have been of great value to him.
He could have made a different request for every one of
the 700 he wanted to remember.

More than that, he could have made a different request for each of those missionaries day after day, without repeating the same request, until over two years had elapsed!

Two years ago I adopted a plan to pray for the people of the church I pastor, individually and specifically, at least once a week. I took the directory of our members and divided the names into several groups with the plan to pray for one group on Monday, another on Tuesday, and so forth, until each member was remembered during the week.

But soon my praying became quite routine and not very inspirational. It took the form of: "Bless John—help him today. . . . Bless Paul—give him victory today. . . . Bless Mary—minister to her needs today," etc. My praying was quite repetitious. I was fulfilling my resolution to pray for my people, but I honestly didn't enjoy that prayer period very much. My praying was dutiful rather than enjoyable. It was difficult to think of something different for each one.

Then I discovered a pattern that made "praying for others" a thrilling, stimulating, inspirational time. I was reading Paul's epistles and I noticed several ways he prayed for the believers in Ephesus, Colosse, Philippi, etc., and I thought: *I'm going to use some of these same requests as I pray for my people.*

That's the way it started. I wrote down many of these Pauline requests, and adapted them a little for my use. Then with a church directory in one hand and the requests (culled from the New Testament) in the other hand (and with my eyes open), I prayed for my people. Soon I became excited over the way these requests from the first century fit people living in the twentieth century!

This plan revolutionized my personal prayer life. Now I enjoy and thrill in the ministry of praying for others. Let's trust this approach will have a similar result in your life.

The practical way to use this book is with your own prayer lists. Not many will make a list of 700 missionaries the way Henry Woolnough did, but you all undoubtedly have prayer lists . . . names of loved ones, members of your church, missionaries, pastors, evangelists, unsaved people, backslidden folk, government leaders, neighbors, etc. Then you'll have the thrill of "matching" the people on your lists with the requests in this book. Thus you will be praying for them . . . or praising the Lord for them . . . in an individual, specific, biblical way.

Sometimes the "matching" isn't appropriate, in which case simply proceed to another request farther down the list.

May the Lord's richest blessing be *heaped* upon you as you pray for others.

Rejoicing in Christ,
Robert C. Savage

P.S. You might occasionally like to have three things in front of you as you pray: this book, the prayer list you use, and the New Testament.

Read from your Bible the verse on which the request is based. Perhaps you would paraphrase or adapt that verse differently than I have done. By making the comparison, you will meditate on that verse and a rich blessing will accrue. Try it!

4:4   Give _____ victory over every temptation and technique Satan would use to defeat him/her. Just as you, Lord, quoted verses from the Word of God to resist the devil, help _____ to have a working knowledge of the Bible so he/she can do likewise.

4:10   Lord, when you were tempted in the wilderness, you commanded Satan, "Get out of here! Get you hence!" Help _____ to resist the devil with that kind of firmness.

4:19   Make of _____ a fisher of men . . . willing to leave his/her nets to follow you.

5:3, 5, 7   Lord, you taught us that the humble people (the poor in spirit) are blessed . . . likewise those who are meek and merciful. Give to _____ these characteristics: humility, meekness, and mercy.

5:6   May _____ hunger and thirst for righteousness.

5:8, 9   I request two things for _____ . First, that he/she be pure in heart, and second, that he/she be a peacemaker.

5:13   Lord, you taught us that we are the salt of the earth. The purpose of salt is: to preserve, to give flavor, and to purify. Help _____ to be salt in our community, doing what he/she can to preserve this area from corruption and moral rottenness.

5:14, 16 Lord, you taught us that we are the light of the world. Help _____ to let his/her light so shine that others may see his/her good works and glorify you.

5:48 Lord, you commanded, "Be perfect, complete, mature." May it be so with _____ .

6:2 Give _____ victory over seeking the praise of people. Help him/her to be ready to give to the Lord's work without expecting any recognition from others.

6:6, 7 May _____ be a man/woman of prayer . . . praying in secret and avoiding vain repetitions.

6:11-13 I request three things for _____ . First, deliver him/her from evil; second, forgive his/her sins; and third, help him/her to forgive any who have wronged him/her.

6:11 Supply all the material needs _____ has.

6:19 Help _____ not to lay up treasures on earth, but rather to lay up treasures in heaven.

6:24 Lord, we simply can't serve two masters. May _____ not try to do so.

6:25, 28, 31 Lord, you told us not to be anxious about what to eat, what to drink, or what to wear. Enable _____ to conquer these desires.

6:33 Help _____ to seek above all else your will, your kingdom, your righteousness, because then all other material needs will automatically be added unto him/her.

6:34 Help _____ not to worry about tomorrow, but simply to trust that the things of tomorrow will take care of themselves.

7:1 Cure _____ of the tendency to judge others.

7:7 As concerns prayer, Lord, you have told us that when we ask . . . it shall be given us; when we seek . . . we shall find; when we knock . . . it will be opened to us. Teach _____ this blessed promise.

7:12 Lord, you've told us that whatever we want people to do for us, we should do for them. May _____ learn and practice this.

7:24 Open the ears of _____ to hear your sayings. But more than that . . . may he/she *do them,* for this is true wisdom.

8:26 Give _____ victory over all fear. Also, may he/she have *big* faith, not little faith.

10:19 Teach _____ how to respond when he/she is questioned concerning the Christian faith.

10:30, 31 How amazing is your care for us, Lord. You have even numbered the hairs of our heads. Help _____ to rejoice in this and to have greater faith and confidence in you, completely trusting you.

10:37 May _____ love you more than anybody —even more than he/she loves the members of his/her family.

10:38 Give _____ the desire to take up his/her cross and follow you . . . otherwise he/she is not worthy of you.

11:28 Teach _____ the importance of two things: First, to bring to you his/her burdens; and second, to take your yoke upon him/her. In this way, he/she will find rest for his/her soul.

12:36, 37 Lord, by our words we are either justified or condemned. So give _____ the victory over speaking idle words.

13:21 May _____ not be dismayed or give up when tribulation or trials afflict him/her. Give him/her a solid faith with deep roots.

13:23 I want to ask three things for _____ . First, that he/she will sincerely hear the Word; second, that he/she will understand it; and third, that he/she will bear fruit (be it a hundredfold, sixty, or thirty).

14:27 Lord, out on the Sea of Galilee during the storm, you called out to the disciples, "Be of good cheer. It is I. Be not afraid!" Give this same command to _____ and may he/she be obedient to it.

15:8 Lord, many people draw nigh to you with their mouths and honor you with their lips, but their hearts are far from you. May this not be true of _____ .

16:24 Lord, you have told us, "If any man would come after me, let him deny himself and take up his cross and follow me." These are your requirements for discipleship. May _____ be willing and ready to become your disciple.

18:3, 4 You have told us, Lord, that if we want to be great in the kingdom of heaven, we must have the humility of a little child. Give to _____ that kind of humility.

18:6 Keep _____ from being a stumblingblock . . . a disappointment to boys and girls. May these young lives see in him/her an example of genuine Christianity.

18:21, 22 Enable _____ to forgive those who have sinned against him/her . . . even forgiving them 490 times.

19:17-19 The rich young ruler could say he had kept all ten commandments, including honoring and respecting his parents. May _____ likewise obey all these.

19:29 Give to _____ such a complete yieldedness to you that he/she would be willing to forsake home, possessions, and loved ones in order to follow you.

20:26, 27 Lord, you taught us that any who desire to be great or chief in a group must be a servant to others. May _____ have this willingness.

21:6 Lord, we read that the disciples went and *did* as you commanded them. May this be true of _____ .

21:21, 22 Give _____ victory over doubts. May he/she have the confidence and faith that whatever we ask in prayer, believing, we shall receive.

22:9, 10 Help _____ to be willing to go out into the highways and byways to invite people to come to you.

22:37, 38 Lord, you taught us that the greatest commandment is to love you with all our heart, soul, and mind. This is a very difficult order, but help _____ to purpose in his/her heart to do this.

23:5 Give _____ victory over the temptation of doing good deeds in order to be seen of men and to obtain their praise.

23:11, 12 Lord, you taught us that true greatness is achieved by serving others . . . that the humble shall be exalted. Give to _____ this Christ-like spirit.

23:18 Some people appear to be very righteous, but within they are full of hypocrisy. Help _____ to be genuine . . . inside and out.

24:4 Our world is full of deceit and false teachers. Defend _____ , Lord, from all this.

24:12 I pray that _____'s love for you will not wax cold. May he/she have the strength and perseverance to endure to the end.

17

24:42, 44   Lord, in such an hour as we think not, you will return. Help _____ to be ready . . . waiting and watching for your return.

25:20, 21   Lord, to those who faithfully use their talents, you will say: "Well done, good and faithful servant. You have been faithful in a few things. I will make you ruler over many things. Enter into the joy of your Lord." May _____ use his/her talents in such a way that he/she will receive that commendation one day.

25:34-36   Exhort _____ to give food to the hungry and drink to the thirsty.

25:34-36   Inspire _____ to be hospitable to the homeless; to give clothing to the destitute; and to visit the sick and those in prison.

26:41   Exhort _____ to watch and pray and thus build a defense against temptation.

28:10   Give _____ freedom from fear and a desire to "go and tell" others about the Lord.

28:19   Your Great Commission is that we go . . . teach . . . and baptize. Help _____ to know what his/her part is in this commission and then obey it.

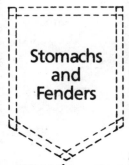

Stomachs and Fenders

Have you ever tried to analyze what people pray for most often in church meetings? You'll probably discover (as I have) that a majority of prayers deal either with . . . *stomachs* or *fenders!*

Many of our prayers (perhaps 70 percent of them) are for the sick (stomach ailments, appendicitis, emphysema, etc.). Another very common request is, "And get us all safely to our homes following this service" (which means "may we not have any damaged fenders to our nice cars").

Prayers for stomachs and fenders are perfectly OK . . . there's nothing wrong with them. God is greatly interested in physical needs and safety on our highways, but aren't there things far more important? Why give the top priority to "stomachs" and "fenders"?

Let's put more stress on the spiritual health of our friends, our loved ones, our fellow church members, and ourselves. That's what the requests of these pages stress. By using these suggestions you'll place less importance on "stomachs" and "fenders" and more emphasis on such things as . . . love, joy, peace, patience, kindness, goodness, faith, meekness, and self-control.

1:37 Your Word tells us "with God nothing shall be impossible." Give to _____ this assurance/confidence.

1:41, 67 Elisabeth and Zacharias were both filled with the Holy Spirit. May _____ likewise be filled with the Holy Spirit.

1:46, 47 May _____ worship you like Mary, saying, "My soul magnifies the Lord, and my spirit rejoices in God my Savior."

1:49 May _____ exalt you as did Mary, saying, "He who is mighty has done great things for me, and holy is his name."

1:64 Of Zacharias we read, "His mouth was opened and his tongue loosed, and he spoke, blessing God." May it be that way with _____ .

1:79 A responsibility of John the Baptist was to give light to those who sit in darkness; and to guide their feet into the way of peace. Use _____ as a witness for you in a similar way.

2:20 After seeing the Christ child in Bethlehem, the shepherds returned to their fields, glorifying and praising God for all they had heard and seen. Fill _____'s heart likewise with an overflow of praise to you.

2:40, 52 As a boy, Jesus grew physically; he waxed strong in spirit; and he was filled with wisdom, and the grace of God was upon him. These same characteristics can be ours. May it be so in the life of _____ .

4:4-13 Lord, help _____ to learn from your example how to resist temptation. Give him/her a knowledge of the Bible to be able to defeat Satan with quotes, "As it is written. . . ."

4:16 May _____ have the same custom the Lord had, namely to be in the house of God each week for worship and reading of the Scriptures.

5:4 Lord, you have called _____ to be a "fisher of men." Help him/her to: launch out into the deep (not lingering along the shore); and may he/she be blessed with a net full of fish.

5:26 When the people observed your mighty works (such as healing the man lowered through the roof), they were amazed and glorified God. May _____ have similar responses in worshiping you.

5:27, 28 Lord, when you spoke to Levi saying, "Follow me," he got up, left all, and followed you. May _____ be ready and willing to do the same.

6:20, 21 Teach _____ four things: first, that our rewards will be given us in the life to come; second, that your kingdom is for the poor; third, that the hungry will be filled; and fourth that those who weep will then laugh.

6:22 May _____ learn to rejoice despite adversity and opposition. Teach him/her that great is the reward in heaven for those who suffer trials and persecution here on earth.

6:27, 35 Help _____ to achieve a maturity in Christ, enabling him/her to love his/her enemies; to do good to them who hate him/her; and to realize that his/her reward will be great.

6:31 Exhort _____ to do unto others as he/she would have others do to him/her.

6:37 Give _____ victory over judging and condemning . . . and may he/she have the spirit of forgiveness, realizing that if we forgive we will be forgiven.

6:38 Lord, you have commanded us, "Give, and it shall be given unto you; good measure, pressed down, shaken together, and running over." You have told us that with the same measure we give it will be given to us again. May _____ put into practice this command and principle.

6:41, 42 Give _____ victory over emphasizing the weaknesses and sins of other people, while ignoring his/her own weaknesses and sins. Help him/her to first cast out the beam that is in his/her own eye and then he/she will see clearly to pull out the mote that is in the eye of another.

6:43-45 Lord, a tree is known by its fruit. So are we. May the life of _____ bring forth good fruit. Out of the abundance of the heart the mouth speaks.

6:46-49 You ask, "Why do you call me Lord and do not the things I say?" If we hear and do what you say we will be like a man who built his house on a rock. In light of this, impress upon _____ the need to *do* what you tell him/her to do.

8:3 Joanna and Susanna ministered to the Lord of their substance (contributed financially to support the work of the Lord). May _____ do this.

8:13 The seed that fell on *stones* represents those who receive the Word with joy, but have no root; for awhile they believe, but when temptation comes they fall away. Oh Lord, give to _____ depth and rootage to his/her faith.

8:14 The seed that fell among *thorns* represents those who hear the Word but are choked with the cares, riches, and pleasures of this world. Oh Lord, may that not happen to _____ .

8:15 May _____ be like the seed that fell on *good ground*. Having heard the Word, help him/her to persist/keep at it and bring forth fruit.

8:16 May _____ not hide his/her faith. May he/she let his/her light shine so that many might be enlightened and glorify you.

8:39 Lord, you told the Gadarene, "Return to your home, to tell them of the great things God has done for you." Give this same command to _____ and enable him/her to go forth and witness to the whole town.

9:23 Lord, you told us, "If any man will come after me, let him deny himself and take up his cross daily and follow me." May _____ be willing and ready to do this.

9:26 Lord, if we are ashamed of you, you will be ashamed of us. Teach _____ this lesson. May he/she be proud of you and his/her faith in you.

9:46-48 Teach _____ how to be great in your estimation. Help him/her to have the humility and trust of a little child.

9:62 Give to _____ the right priorities. Help him/her not to look back, but to keep on keeping on in facing future needs and challenges.

10:2 Lord, you told us that the harvest truly is great and plentiful, but the laborers are few, and that we should pray for more laborers to be sent forth into the fields of harvest. I pray that _____ will respond to the need and get in on the harvesting.

10:33-37   May _____ be a twentieth-century Good Samaritan, having compassion on those who have fallen into difficult situations, lifting them up and caring for them.

10:42   May _____ choose "the one thing that is needful," namely food for the soul rather than food for the stomach.

11:28   Your Word teaches, "Blessed are they that hear the Word of God and keep it." May this be the case in the life of _____ .

11:34-36   Purify the eyes of _____ . Pure eyes will let sunshine into his/her soul; lustful eyes shut out the light and plunge an individual into darkness.

11:39   The Pharisees were specialists in producing cleanliness on the outside, but on the inside they were dirty, full of greed and wickedness. Spare _____ from that.

11:42   The Pharisees were faithful in tithing their income, but neglected justice and love. May _____ imitate them in the matter of tithing, but not leave the other things undone.

12:2   Lord, there is nothing about our lives that is covered or that shall not be revealed—nothing hid that shall not be made known. May _____ live his/her life recognizing this.

12:6, 7   Teach _____ the truths concerning your amazing love and watch-care for us . . . that you have numbered the hairs of our heads. Teach him/her that your eye is on every sparrow and that we are of more value than many sparrows.

12:8 May _____ be proud to confess you before others.

12:12 May _____ rely on the Holy Spirit to teach him/her what to say in any and every situation.

12:15 Warn _____ to beware of greed and coveting, for a man's life consists not in the abundance of the things he possesses.

12:21 Give _____ the victory over desires to lay up for himself/herself treasures. Rather, may he/she aspire to be rich toward God.

12:22, 23 Give _____ the right priorities. Help him/her not to be preoccupied with food and clothing.

12:27 Lord, we are told that if God takes care of lilies, how much more will he care for us. Give _____ this faith and confidence.

12:29-31 Lord, it's difficult to obey your command: "Don't worry about food, what to eat and drink." But at least help _____ not to put priorities on these, but simply trust you to supply them.

12:32 Relieve _____ of all fear.

12:33 Give to _____ the willingness to sell possessions and give to those in need. This will fatten his/her purse in heaven.

12:35-40 May _____ be prepared and ready for your return.

12:48 Lord, much has been given _____ . Help him/her to realize that "to whom much is given, of him will much be required."

13:6, 7 Lord, just as the owner of the fig tree expected to find fruit on the tree, likewise you expect *us* to bear fruit. Impress this upon _____ and teach him/her that we must not be like the fig tree (spiritually barren) and that we bring joy to you in proportion to the fruit we produce.

14:11   Teach _____ that everyone who tries to honor himself shall be humbled; and he who humbles himself shall be honored.

14:13   Give to _____ a special compassion for the poor, the crippled, the lame, and the blind.

14:26   Lord, impress upon _____ that anyone who wants to be your follower must love you more than father, mother, wife, children, brothers, or sisters. Otherwise we cannot be your disciples.

14:33   You taught us, Lord, that no one can become your disciple unless he is willing to renounce all he has. May _____ learn this truth.

15:4-7   Give to _____ a spirit of rejoicing and excitement about sinners who repent, concerning the lost sheep that has been found. May he/she be willing and longing to win at least one soul to Christ.

15:11-24   (For the backslidden.) Lord, _____ has wandered away from you and has gotten all mixed up in various sinful activities. Heal his/her backsliding and may he/she resolve to "come back home."

15:25-32   Sometimes, Lord, faithful Christians become jealous of the attention given to restored backsliders. Free _____ of any such feelings and may he/she join in the rejoicing and celebration when a prodigal son or daughter comes back home.

16:10   Teach _____ that we must be honest in small matters, otherwise we won't be honest in large ones . . . that if we cheat even a little bit, we can't be trusted with greater responsibilities.

27

16:13   Teach _____ the right attitude about money, that he/she cannot serve both God and money, ... that loving money will result in lack of fervor for serving you.

16:15   Lord, you know all about us. You know whether there is pretense in us to obtain honor and commendation from people. Cleanse _____ of this and help him/her to recognize that often what is exalted among men is an abomination in your sight.

17:3, 4   Give to _____ the spirit of forgiveness ... the willingness to forgive a repentant person many times each day.

17:15, 16   Just as one leper (when he was healed) glorified God with a loud voice and prostrated himself to give you thanks, may a similar spirit of thanksgiving and gratitude fill _____ .

18:9, 14   Cleanse _____ of self-righteousness and spiritual pride ... for everyone who exalts himself will be humbled, and he who humbles himself will be exalted.

18:16   Give _____ the right attitude toward children ... encouraging them and inviting them to come to Jesus.

18:22   May _____ be willing to make financial sacrifices in following you, knowing this will result in receiving a wonderful treasure in heaven.

18:27   Impress upon _____ that the things which are impossible with men are possible with you.

18:28-30   May _____ be like Peter ... ready to leave all to follow you, realizing that he/she will be rewarded in this life and also will receive eternal life in the world to come.

19:17 Lord, you have given all of us certain talents, and you expect us to use them wisely. May _____ be a good and faithful servant. May his/her life produce dividends for your honor and glory. May he/she realize the reward of ruling with you will be given to those who serve you faithfully.

19:37 At the triumphal entry the multitude rejoiced and praised God (with a loud voice) for all the mighty works they had seen. Give to _____ a similar spirit of exuberant praise and worship.

20:25 Give to _____ a twofold spirit of obedience . . . rendering to human authorities what corresponds to them and rendering to you the things which are of God.

21:2-4 May _____ be generous in giving to the work of the Lord . . . similar to the widow who gave her two mites.

21:12, 14, 15 If and when _____ faces opposition or persecution, give him/her calmness and steadfastness, completely trusting you to provide wisdom which enemies of the gospel will not be able to contradict or resist.

21:28, 36 Lord, perhaps our redemption is drawing very near and your return will soon occur. In view of this, may _____ be waiting and watching. Help him/her to look up and lift up his/her eyes.

21:34 Lord, you told us, "Take heed lest that day come upon you unexpectedly." May _____ be very mindful of that warning.

22:26 Help _____ to be willing to serve others, rather than wanting to exercise authority.

24:45 Lord, when you met with the disciples after your resurrection, you opened their understanding concerning the Scriptures. I pray that you will do the same for _____ .

24:48 Just as the disciples became witnesses of what the Lord had done, may _____ be a witness of what you have done in our day.

24:49 You promised the disciples they would be endued with power from on high. Give to _____ this same power from on high.

24:53 After your ascension the disciples were continually in the Temple, praising and blessing God. May _____ follow their example.

Earthquakes

Have you ever been in an earthquake?

On August 5, 1949, we had a devastating quake in Ecuador. We felt some strong tremors in Quito, even though the center of intensity was seventy-five miles away (in Ambato).

My, how people cry out to the Lord when they feel a tremor—when the pictures on the wall start to sway and the walls of their house seem about ready to crack. "Oh, God, spare me! Help me! Protect me from the collapsing ceiling and roof!" More than 5,000 died in a few short minutes. Other thousands suddenly became men and women of urgent prayer.

You would think those who were spared would continue to seek the Lord and be contrite before him. But it doesn't always work that way. When the tremors cease and the noise quits, there are sighs of relief and, expressed or unexpressed, the attitude is, "Whew! I'm sure glad it didn't get me. Lord, good-bye for now—I'll be calling on you again the next time there is a quake!"

That's not prayer! It is an insult to God to only seek him when there is an emergency (times of danger, sickness, financial need, etc.).

4:21-24 Teach _____ how to worship you in spirit and in truth rather than with candles, statues, robes, etc. And reveal to him/her that the important thing is not the *place* of worship but the *manner* of worship.

4:35 Lord, lost souls are all around us, like fields ripe and ready for reaping. Help _____ to lift up his/her eyes to see this challenge and get involved in the harvesting.

4:36-38 Lord, you assign some to be sowers and some to be reapers. May _____ know which is his/her job—then help him/her to faithfully fulfill it.

5:24 (For the unsaved.) May _____ sincerely listen to the message of salvation and then fully trust you. In this way he/she can be assured of everlasting life . . . passing from death unto life.

5:39; 7:52 May _____ be one who searches the Scriptures.

6:27 May _____ be primarily concerned about spiritual food for his/her soul rather than for perishable food for the stomach.

7:18 May _____ not look for praise for himself/herself, but rather seek to honor you.

7:38, 39 Inasmuch as _____ believes in you, and has received the Holy Spirit, may joy and love like rivers of living water flow from his/her heart to bless many.

8:12 Lord, you are the light of the world. Help _____ to follow you faithfully, so he/she won't be stumbling through darkness.

8:31 Make of _____ a genuine disciple. This means that he/she must hold fast to your teachings, and do so continuously.

8:32 Lord, freedom is a precious possession. But we are never really free until we know the truth. Give to _____ this kind of freedom.

8:34-36 Lord, you taught us that if we commit and practice sin, we are slaves to sin. Emancipate _____ so that he/she will be free indeed from sin.

9:7 Lord, the blind man went where you sent him. May _____ do the same.

10:4, 5, 27 Sheep recognize the shepherd's voice and daily follow *him* . . . not a stranger. May that be the pattern for _____ , faithfully following you and refusing to follow anyone except you.

11:41 Teach _____ how to give you thanks for answered prayer . . . even before the answer comes.

12:3 May _____ be ready to give his/her *very best* to Jesus.

12:13 May _____'s heart be filled with joyful, spontaneous "Hosannas"—praising you sincerely.

12:25, 26 May the purpose of _____'s life be to follow you and only you. May he/she even be willing to lose his/her life as a price for devotion and loyalty to the Lord.

12:43 Spare _____ from loving the praise of men more than the praise of God.

13:14, 15 Give to _____ the same humility and condescension you had Lord, when you stooped to wash the dirty feet of the disciples.

13:34, 35; 15:17 Give to _____ a deep love for other Christians. The unsaved will know we are Christians by our love for each other.

14:1 Free _____ from worry and fear. Don't let his/her heart be troubled.

14:13, 14; 16:23, 24 Teach _____ the blessed promise about prayer . . . that we can ask you, Father, for anything in the name of Jesus and you will do it.

14:15, 21, 24 Lord, it is one thing to *say* we love you and quite another to *really* obey you and keep your commandments. May _____ prove his/her love for you by *full obedience*.

14:27; 16:33 Lord, you promised to leave us a wonderful gift—namely, peace. May this peace fill the mind and heart of _____ .

15:2, 5, 8 Lord, we should be bearing fruit, reproducing Christians. This is the way you are glorified. Give _____ the desire to bear much fruit for your honor and glory, and then provide him/her with the ability to do so.

15:2 Sometimes, Lord, we need pruning so we can bear more fruit. If _____ needs your pruning, help him/her to realize that it is all for the best.

15:11; 16:24 Pour out upon _____ your joy, and may that joy be like a cup full and overflowing.

17:15, 17 Keep _____ from evil and sanctify him/her through your Word. Your Word is truth.

20:26, 27 May _____ have your peace and not be doubting but rather believing.

21:17 May _____ truly love you with an *"agape"* love and be used to feed your lambs and sheep.

What Is Your Number One Request?

When Solomon became King of Israel, God gave him the opportunity to make any request —anything! Solomon's Number One request was for *wisdom* . . . and God gave it to him.

Question: If the Lord would give *you* the same opportunity he gave Solomon, what would be *your* Number One request? Would it be the same as Solomon's—a request for wisdom?

Proverbs 4:5 (KJV) tells us: "Get wisdom, get understanding; forget it not; neither decline from the words of my mouth."

Proverbs 4:5, 6 (TLB) exhorts: "Learn to be wise . . . and develop good judgment and common sense! I cannot overemphasize this point. Cling to wisdom—she will protect you. Love her—she will guard you."

Personally, I try to begin every day asking the Lord for wisdom in every decision I'll be called upon to make during the day. But if the Lord should give me the same opportunity he gave Solomon, I would *not* make *wisdom* my Number One request. Rather I would ask the Lord for the characteristic so frequently mentioned in the book of Acts, namely: to be full of the Holy Spirit.

Why don't you check Acts 2:4; 4:8, 31; 6:5; 7:55; and Ephesians 5:18?

Remember, there can and should be *many fillings* of the Spirit—not just one. I believe it is perfectly in order to pray *every day* for a new filling of the Holy Spirit. In fact, that is my Number One request of God each day—for myself.

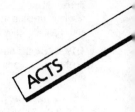

1:8 Give _____ the desire and power to be a witness everywhere. May the Holy Spirit come upon him/her to provide this power.

2:17 We have your promise, Lord, "I will pour out my Holy Spirit upon all mankind. Your sons and daughters shall prophesy. Your young men shall see visions, and your old men will dream dreams. The Holy Spirit shall come upon all my servants, men and women alike." I pray that this promise will be fulfilled in the life of _____ .

2:25 Help _____ to confidently say with King David, "I know the Lord is always with me. He is helping me. God's mighty power supports me."

2:26 May _____'s heart be filled with joy and may his/her tongue shout your praises.

2:38 (For the unsaved.) Just as Peter exhorted the multitudes to repent and be baptized in the name of Jesus Christ, I pray that _____ will do likewise.

2:42 The Jerusalem Christians met together regularly for teaching sessions, prayer meetings, and the observance of the Lord's Supper. I pray that _____ will follow that example.

2:45 Give to _____ a generous heart . . . and may he/she be willing to sell his/her possessions to help those in need.

2:46 May _____ imitate those early Christians by regularly meeting in the house of God to worship you and enjoy the fellowship of other Christians.

3:19 (For the unsaved.) I pray for _____ that he/she might repent and be converted. Blot out his/her sins.

4:8-12 Because he was filled with the Holy Spirit, Peter could witness with power concerning salvation in Jesus Christ. May _____ likewise be filled with the Spirit and be able to witness with power.

4:13 May it be possible for people to look upon _____ and declare, "We perceive that he/she has been with Jesus."

4:20 May _____ be so zealous for the Lord that he/she will say, "I simply cannot help but tell others about what I have seen and heard."

4:31 May _____ be filled with the Holy Spirit and be able to speak the word of God with all boldness.

5:28 The early Christians were accused of filling all Jerusalem with Christian teaching. Enable us to do the same thing in our town, and may _____ greatly help in fulfilling this.

5:29 Peter and the apostles had the conviction, "We must obey God rather than men." May _____ have a similar conviction.

6:3 May _____ be full of wisdom and also full of the Holy Spirit.

6:8 Stephen was full of *faith* and full of *power*. Fill _____ also with faith and with power.

8:4 We are told that the believers went everywhere preaching the Good News about Jesus. Give _____ this kind of zeal.

8:37, 38 (For those not baptized.) Lord, if _____ believes in Jesus with all his/her heart, give him/her the desire to be baptized.

9:6 May _____ follow the example of Saul of Tarsus, asking, "Lord, what will you have me do?" Then may he/she *do it!*

9:31 The believers learned how to walk in the fear of the Lord and in the comfort of the Holy Spirit. Help _____ to learn this same pattern.

9:36 Help _____ to follow the example of Dorcas by doing kind things for others, especially for the poor.

10:2 We read that Cornelius was a godly man, deeply reverent. He gave generously to those in need and was a man of prayer. May _____ have these same characteristics.

10:33 May _____ be ready to hear and receive all things you would instruct and teach him/her.

10:45 May the Holy Spirit be poured out upon _____ .

10:48 (For those not baptized.) May _____ desire to be baptized in the name of the Lord.

11:23 May _____ stay close to you; may he/she remain faithful to you and be devoted to you . . . with steadfast purpose of heart.

11:24 May _____ be like Barnabas—a good man (person) . . . full of the Holy Spirit and full of faith.

13:48, 49 Help _____ to rejoice and give thanks for the Word of God. May he/she do much to help spread that Word throughout all the region.

13:52 May _____ be filled with joy and also filled with the Holy Spirit.

16:6, 7   May _____ be directed at all times by the Holy Spirit, knowing when to "go" and when to "wait," and when to change plans entirely.

17:6, 7   Lord, we read that the Christians of the first century "turned the world upside down." We need to do this today. May _____ help achieve that goal.

17:11   May _____ be like the people in Berea, receiving the Word of God with all readiness of mind, and searching the Scriptures daily.

18:9, 10   Lord, speak to _____ in the same way you spoke to Paul, saying, "Don't be afraid! Speak out! Don't quit! For I am with you and no one can harm you."

18:24, 25   May _____ be like Apollos, instructed in the way of the Lord and fervent in spirit.

19:20   May the word of God grow mightily (and prevail) in the life of _____ .

20:24   May _____ have the dedication of Paul, saying, "I consider my life as worth nothing unless I use it to finish the race and complete the task assigned me by the Lord Jesus—the work of telling others the gospel of God's grace."

20:35   Lord, you have taught us that it is "more blessed to give than to receive." May _____ follow that principle.

22:15   May _____ be a witness of your power and truth to everybody.

23:11   May _____ be of good cheer today.

26:16   Enable _____ to "stand up for Jesus" in all situations and be a witness for the Lord . . . telling others what he/she has experienced in Christ.

26:18 Lord, use _____ to bless many, especially the unsaved—to open their eyes and turn them from darkness to light, and from the power of Satan to God.

27:25 May _____ be of good cheer and fully trust you (even in the most adverse circumstances).

28:31 Give to _____ the talent of teaching with all confidence the truths concerning the Lord Jesus.

A Bushel of Hershey Bars

Sometimes we think of prayer as a way to get *my* will done! No! Prayer is a means of getting *his* will done! And let's not forget: getting *his* will done is precisely the best thing that can ever happen to *me!* It isn't best for me to get my will done. What will bring me the very highest, greatest, most supreme joy is to get his will done.

The story is told of a wealthy woman whose small boy was a brat . . . very spoiled. A teenage girl was caring for the little guy one afternoon, while the mother was in another part of the house.

A wasp flew into the room and the boy saw its brilliant colors. He began calling, "I want it! I want it!"

The mother, not knowing what he meant, called from the other room, "Let the boy have what he wants. Let him have it!" And the baby-sitter complied. She let him have it.

Soon the wealthy mother heard a loud, anguished scream. She called out, "What's the matter?" The girl simply answered, "He got what he wanted."

Often God doesn't give us what we want. But he always gives us what is *best* for us. Perhaps we ask God for something that obviously is *not* good for us. For example, I could pray, "Dear God, please give me a bushel of Hershey bars!" God knows very well that if I ate a bushel of Hershey bars I would die of indigestion.

But many times we ask him for something just as ridiculous and then we tack on the pious phrase, "if it be thy will." Remember, prayer is not getting *my* will done, but rather getting *God's* will done.

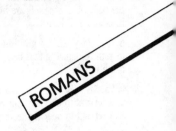

1:14-16 May _____ never be ashamed of the gospel of Christ. Rather may he/she be ready to share it with others in every way possible. Help him/her to realize we are debtors to the unsaved.

2:7 May _____ be primarily concerned in seeking your glory, your honor, and eternal rewards rather than earthly honors.

2:16 Lord, we know the day will come when you will judge our secret lives, our inmost thoughts. This will include _____ . So help him/her to live each day recognizing this and preparing for it.

4:20 May _____ like Abraham believe you completely without wavering. May he/she be strengthened in faith and give you the glory.

5:1, 2 Give to _____ a spirit of rejoicing because he/she has been justified by faith, and also has peace with God; plus he/she has access into grace, and the anticipation of sharing your glory. This is great, Lord! Amen! Hallelujah!

5:3-5 Lord, give _____ the maturity to rejoice when trials come; knowing that trials are good for us (they develop patience in us); and patience develops strength of character and hope.

6:12   Lord, I pray that sin shall no longer reign in the body of _____ . Spare him/her from yielding to lusts and evil desires.

6:13   May _____ give himself/herself completely to you, recognizing that he/she has been brought from death to life.

6:16, 18   Help _____ not to yield himself/herself as a servant to obey sin, but rather yield himself/herself as a servant to obey righteousness.

6:19   Just as _____ formerly yielded the members of his/her body to impurity and wickedness, may he/she now yield the members of his/her body to righteousness and holiness.

6:22   O Lord, _____ has been set free from the power of sin and is now your servant, your slave. May he/she manifest this by a life of holiness.

8:4   Help _____ not to walk after the flesh, but after the Spirit. May he/she not live according to our sinful nature but rather submit to the Holy Spirit and follow him.

8:5, 6   Help _____ to no longer have his/her mind set on things our sinful nature desires, but rather on what the Holy Spirit desires.

8:9-14   Blessed Holy Spirit, you dwell in _____ . May he/she be constantly led and guided by you in all ways.

8:18   Help _____ to realize that the sufferings of the present time are not worthy to be compared with the glory you will give us later.

8:27   Blessed Holy Spirit, _____'s heart is being searched. Is he/she living in harmony with your will? If not, help him/her to completely submit to your will today.

8:28 Give _____ the confidence that all things work together for good because he/she loves you and is called according to your purpose.

8:29 O Father, may _____ sincerely desire to be like Jesus, your Son.

8:31 Give _____ the assurance and confidence that since you are for us, nobody can prevail against us.

8:35, 38, 39 Give to _____ the assurance and confidence that absolutely nothing can separate him/her from your love.

8:37 Make _____ more than a conqueror through Christ who loved us.

9:2, 3 May _____ have a great passion for the unsaved, similar to Paul's passion to see his fellow Jews saved, even ready to be accursed from Christ if this would lead to their salvation.

9:17 O Lord, display your power in the life of _____, and through him/her may your name be published to multitudes.

9:21 May _____ be willing to be a mere "lump of clay" in your hands, ready to be molded as you desire.

10:1 May the heart's desire and prayer of _____ be for the salvation of others.

10:9-11 Give _____ victory over timidity. Help him/her to not be ashamed of the gospel. May he/she be proud to confess with his/her mouth Jesus as Lord.

11:20, 22 Keep _____ from being arrogant or high-minded. Give him/her a humble fear of God and may he/she continue to love and trust you.

12:1 May _____ present his/her body to you as a living sacrifice—eyes, ears, hands, feet, tongue, and heart all sacrificed to you. This is the reasonable way to worship.

12:2 May _____ not be conformed to the pattern of this world, but be transformed by the renewing of his/her mind.

12:2 I pray that above all else _____ might seek your good and acceptable and perfect will.

12:3 Help _____ not to think of himself/herself more highly than he/she ought to think, and be honest in his/her estimate of himself/herself.

12:6-8 May _____ faithfully use the gifts you have given him/her.

12:9 Teach _____ to abhor all that is evil and cling to that which is good.

12:10 May _____ be kindly affectioned toward others with brotherly love . . . in honor preferring *others* rather than himself/herself.

12:11 May _____ not be lacking in zeal . . . and may he/she be fervent in spirit in serving you.

12:12 I request three things for _____ . Help him/her to rejoice in our hope; to be patient in affliction; and to continue to be faithful in prayer.

12:13 May _____ share with God's people who have material needs.

12:15 Give to _____ a sympathetic, compassionate spirit to rejoice with those who rejoice and weep with those who weep.

12:16 May _____ live in harmony with others. May he/she not seek "high things" (try to act big). Instead, may he/she be willing to fellowship with people of low position and not be conceited (thinking he/she knows it all).

12:17 Eliminate vindictiveness from _____ . Help him/her not to repay others with evil for evil.

12:17 Help _____ to provide things honest in the sight of everybody, so that they can see he/she is transparently sincere.

12:18 As far as possible, help _____ to live peaceably with all others, not quarreling with anyone.

12:19 Help _____ not to be vengeful, but to leave with you the matter of administering justice and punishment.

12:21 Help _____ not to be overcome with evil, but to overcome evil with good.

13:7 Enable _____ to be a law-abiding citizen, rendering tribute to whom tribute is due; giving respect and honor to whom they are due.

13:9, 10 I pray that _____ may obey all the Ten Commandments, but even more important, help him/her to love other people in the same measure that he/she loves himself/herself . . . for love is the fulfillment of the commandments.

13:11, 12 Lord, wake up _____ out of spiritual slumber. Help him/her to cast off the works of darkness and put on the armor of light.

13:13 May _____ walk honestly and uprightly . . . knowing nothing of wild parties, drunkenness, sexual immorality, fighting, or jealousy.

14:1-5 Give _____ the right attitude toward those with different standards of conduct than he/she possesses. Free him/her of spiritual pride.

14:5, 10, 13 Give _____ victory over being judgmental and legalistic. Help him/her to quit judging others. Judging is your job, Lord.

14:19 Help _____ to follow peace. May he/she seek ways to edify others and build them up.

15:1 Help _____ to help others . . . and not try primarily to please himself/herself.

15:5 Teach _____ to live in harmony with others in a spirit of unity.

15:11 May _____'s life be characterized by praise . . . *continually* praising you.

15:13 I pray that you will fill _____ with joy and peace . . . that he/she may abound in hope through the power of the Holy Spirit.

15:14 May _____ be full of goodness; complete in knowledge and competent to instruct others.

Should
We
Kneel?

Many people place a great deal of emphasis on the position of the body when praying. Some insist that you kneel every time you pray or that you fold your hands or lift them in a certain way.

All this is relatively unimportant. Personally, I prefer to kneel when it is possible. But any position is perfectly OK.

Joshua *fell on his face* to worship and pray (Joshua 5:14).

Solomon *stood* before the altar of the Lord . . . and spread forth his hands toward heaven (1 Kings 8:22).

Daniel *knelt* three times a day and prayed, and gave thanks before his God (Daniel 6:10).

We can pray—lying flat on our backs . . . sitting in our chairs . . . driving our cars . . . walking through the woods. Any position is OK.

Once at the Prayer Tower, high on a sand

dune overlooking Lake Michigan at the Maranatha Bible Conference, I was with Evangelist George Stephens in a prayer meeting. I'll never forget how he prostrated himself flat on his face on that wood floor as he called out to the Lord. That was good! But the important thing in prayer is the condition of our heart, not the position of our body.

1:5 Lord, you have enriched the life of _____ . Now help him/her to speak out for you and give him/her a full understanding of the truth.

1:10 Lord, your desire for us is that we be of one mind and be united in thought and purpose . . . that we Christians be perfectly joined together. May _____ fit into that pattern.

1:19, 20 Help _____ not to revere human wisdom and the philosophies of the scholars. Help him/her to realize that you have made them all look foolish and shown worldly wisdom to be useless nonsense.

1:30, 31 If _____ has a desire to boast, may he/she boast only of what you have done, recognizing that Jesus is . . . our wisdom, our righteousness, our sanctification . . . and our redemption.

2:9, 10 Blessed Holy Spirit, you reveal to us things that eyes have not seen, nor have ears heard. Be a revealer to _____ today, showing him/her the deep things of God.

2:15 Help _____ to be a Spirit-filled Christian . . . and have the insight to discern what the non-Christian (the natural man) cannot understand. With this insight, may he/she know what is true or false . . . what is right and what is wrong.

2:16 In every decision _____ makes today, help him/her to have the mind of Christ.

3:2 _____ needs to grow spiritually, advancing beyond the "milk" stage to feeding on solid spiritual food (meat for the soul).

3:3 Give _____ victory over all carnality. May he/she not follow his/her own desires, substituting them for your perfect will. Emancipate him/her from all jealousy and quarreling.

3:10, 11 Lord Jesus, you are the foundation of our lives. There is no other. We must build on that foundation. Help _____ to be very careful how he/she builds.

3:13 There is coming a day of testing to reveal what kind of material we have used in building our lives . . . a testing by fire to prove what sort of work each one has done. Help _____ to live his/her life preparing for that day of judgment.

3:16, 17 Lord, the body of _____ is your temple. Just as a temple should be undefiled and holy, may _____ keep his/her body undefiled and holy.

3:18, 19 Help _____ not to deceive himself/herself into thinking that he/she is wise. May he/she recognize himself/herself as foolish, in order to become really wise. For the wisdom of this world is foolishness with you.

4:2 Lord, the most important thing about a servant is to do just what his master tells him. _____ is your servant. May he/she do exactly what you command.

4:4, 5 Lord, when you return you will turn on the light so that everyone can see what each of us really is, deep down in our hearts. At that time you will give whatever praise we are to receive. Help _____ to live with this prospect in view and be careful not to jump to conclusions beforehand whether someone is a good Christian or not.

4:7 Lord, what is _____ so puffed up about? What does he/she have that you haven't given him/her? And if all is from you, why does he/she act as though he/she is so great, and has accomplished something on his/her own? Help him/her to get rid of this boasting.

4:8 Lord, oftentimes we become proud, feeling we are rich and full and in need of nothing—acting like a king on the throne. Give _____ victory over such temptation.

4:19, 20 May _____ not only *"talk"* a good Christian life, but *live* a life of spiritual power.

6:13, 18 Lord, our bodies are for you and your glory. They are not for fornication. Help _____ to flee from sexual sin.

6:19, 20 Lord, you own our bodies. You have bought us with a great price. Our bodies are the temple of the Holy Spirit. They do not belong to us. So help _____ to glorify you with every part of his/her body.

7:1, 2, 8, 37, 38 (For single people.) Lord, reveal to _____ whether or not he/she should marry. Your Word teaches that in many cases it is better not to marry.

7:3 (For married people.) Help _____ to render to his/her partner the personal rights and privileges involved in marriage, recognizing that one's body is subject to the marital partner.

7:29, 30 Lord, "the time is short" and we need to use it wisely—not placing the emphasis on the comforts and fashions of this world. Impress this upon _____ .

8:1, 2 Your Word tells us "knowledge puffs up, but love builds up." Instead of a "know-it-all" attitude, help _____ to specialize in *love* for you and for others.

8:9, 13 These verses warn us about becoming stumblingblocks to those who are weak in the faith. May there be nothing in _____'s life that will cause others to stumble.

9:11, 13, 14 Help _____ to be generous in supporting the work of the Lord financially.

9:16 Paul said, "Woe to me if I do not preach the gospel." May _____ feel the same way about the job you have given him/her to do.

9:19 In his passion to win the lost, Paul was ready to make himself a slave to everyone and in that way win many to Christ. May _____ have a similar passion.

9:20-22 In his passion to win the lost, Paul declared, "I have become all things to all men so that by all possible means I might save some." Fill the heart of _____ with this zeal.

9:25 Help _____ to be a good spiritual athlete—to get into condition and deny himself/herself the things that would hinder the race.

9:26 Enable _____ to run the Christian race with certainty . . . with a purpose in every step . . . and not be one who is just beating the air.

9:27 Exhort _____ to bring his/her body into subjection . . . training it to do what it should . . . lest he/she become unfit and be disqualified.

10:10 Give _____ victory over grumbling and murmuring.

10:12 May _____ be mindful of your warning, "Let him that thinks he stands, take heed lest he fall."

10:13 Whatever temptation or testing _____ is called upon to bear, help him/her to realize that: First, many others have faced the same thing. Second, you are faithful and will not permit any trial beyond our ability to endure. Third, you promise to provide the way of victory with every temptation.

10:24 Exhort _____ not to think only of himself/herself, but to think of others and their welfare.

10:31 Help _____ to do everything for the glory of God, even his/her eating and drinking.

10:32, 33 Help _____ not to seek his/her own advantage, but to try to do what is most profitable for others, that they may be saved.

12:12-27 May _____ understand how the Holy Spirit has fitted us all together in one body, the body of Christ—and that he/she is a very necessary part of that body.

12:25 Lord, there should be no discord in the body of Christ. All members of the body should have the same care for each other as they have for themselves. Teach _____ this truth.

12:31 Help _____ to earnestly desire the best gifts of the Holy Spirit, especially the gift of love which is better than any of them!

13:1 Show _____ that love for others is far more important than speaking in other languages.

13:2 Show _____ that love for others is far more important than explaining what is going to happen in the future.

13:2 Show _____ that love for others is far more important than a wealth of education (having all knowledge).

13:2 Show _____ that love for others is far more important than the gift of faith (even faith that can make mountains move).

13:3 Show _____ that love for others is far more important than being a philanthropist (bestowing all one's wealth to feed the poor).

13:3 Show _____ that love for others is far more important than willingness to die for Christ as a martyr.

13:4 Love is very patient and kind. May _____ be that way.

13:4 Love is never jealous, boastful, or proud. Eliminate all that in _____ .

13:5 Love is never haughty, selfish, or rude. May _____ have none of that.

13:5 Love does not demand its own way—is not irritable or touchy. Cleanse _____ of all this.

13:5 May the pattern of love be found in _____'s life, recognizing that love does not hold grudges and hardly even notices when others do it wrong.

13:6 May the pattern of love be seen in the life of _____ , recognizing that love is never glad about injustice, but rejoices whenever truth wins out.

13:7 (For married people.) May the pattern of love be evident in _____'s life, recognizing that love bears up under anything and everything that comes along (being loyal to the person you love no matter what the cost).

13:11 Help _____ to put away childish things.

14:12 Bestow upon _____ gifts that will enable him/her to edify and build up others in the church.

14:15 Help _____ , both in praying and singing, to do so intelligently and with understanding.

14:20 May _____ be as an innocent child concerning evil things, but as a mature man/woman of intelligence in solving problems.

14:33, 40 We know, Lord, that you want things done decently, orderly, harmoniously. Help _____ to do things that way.

15:34 Help _____ to wake up to the situations we face, and quit sinning.

15:54-56 Give to _____ the right attitude about death . . . that death is victory for the Christian.

15:58 May _____ be steadfast, unmovable, always abounding in the work of the Lord, knowing that his/her labor is not in vain in the Lord.

16:2 May _____ be faithful about money matters. May he/she contribute generously to your work every Sunday as you have prospered him/her.

16:8, 9 Lord, you have opened great doors of opportunity to _____ . Perhaps there are adversaries who oppose him/her, but help _____ to "stay with it" and not give up.

16:13 Help _____ to watch; to stand fast in the faith; to live courageously; to be strong.

16:14 Whatever _____ does, help him/her to do it with kindness and love.

Three Ways God Answers

Very possibly T. J. Bach was the greatest man of prayer I've ever known. He was the Director of The Evangelical Alliance Mission (TEAM). Often I've heard him explain (in that delightful Danish accent): "There are three ways God answers our prayers: First, 'Yes'; second, 'No'; third, 'Wait just a bit.'"

GALATIANS

1:6 May _____ be firm and steadfast in the faith and not turn away from you to embrace some false teaching.

1:7 Keep _____ from being deceived by those who twist and change the truth concerning Christ.

1:10 Spare _____ from trying to please people with flattery and sweet talk. Rather may he/she always try to please you.

2:20 _____ has been crucified with Christ. Nevertheless he/she lives . . . in fact Christ lives in him/her. Help him/her to manifest this in all he/she does or says.

4:6, 7 We who are your children are heirs of all that belongs to you. What an incredible honor! May _____ conduct himself/herself in the way members of the Royal Family should live.

5:7 (For the lukewarm or backslidden.) Lord, _____ was getting along so well in his/her Christian life, but that isn't true now. Who or what has been hindering him/her? May that influence be eliminated so that _____ will once again be victorious and grow in you.

5:13 Lord, you have given us freedom . . . but not freedom to do wrong; rather freedom to love and serve each other. May _____ use his/her freedom in the right way.

5:17 Lord, a battle between the flesh and the Spirit is being waged in each of us. May _____ be victorious in this conflict, doing what the Spirit indicates.

5:19 Emancipate _____ from the works of the flesh . . . adultery, fornication, impurity.

5:20 May all selfishness, dissension, and false doctrine be eliminated from _____'s life.

5:21 Envy, drunkenness, wild parties and all that sort of thing are works of the flesh. May _____ be entirely freed from these.

5:22 Give to _____ the fruit of the Spirit. Specifically may he/she have love, joy, and peace.

5:22 Patience, gentleness, and goodness are three characteristics of the fruit of the Holy Spirit. May _____ develop these.

5:22, 23 Faith, meekness, and self-control are a part of the fruit of the Holy Spirit. May _____'s life manifest these three.

5:24 May all evil desires and lusts be crucified . . . put to death in the life of _____ .

5:26 Eliminate in _____ vain glory and self-conceit. May he/she not say things that provoke others and produce hard feelings.

6:1 Give to _____ the right attitude concerning any other Christian who has sinned. Help _____ to restore that one in a spirit of meekness, remembering that any of us could be similarly tempted.

6:2 Help _____ to share the troubles and problems of other Christians.

6:3 Lord, if we think ourselves to be something, when in reality we are nothing, we simply deceive ourselves. Save _____ from that.

6:4 May _____ carefully examine and test his/her own conduct and be able to assess properly the value of his/her own work . . . without any need to compare himself/herself with anyone else.

6:7 Help _____ not to be deceived. Help him/her to remember that you are not mocked. None of us can disobey you and get away with it. Remind him/her that whatever he/she sows, that shall he/she also reap.

6:9 Help _____ not to be weary in well doing. Show him/her that if we don't get discouraged and give up, in due time we will reap a harvest of blessing.

6:10 Enable _____ (whenever there is opportunity) to do good to everyone, but especially to our Christian brothers and sisters.

6:14 Help _____ not to boast about anything except the cross of our Lord Jesus. Because of that cross may the attraction and tug of the world be crucified . . . dead for him/her.

Long or Short Prayers?

I remember an all-night prayer meeting with Peter Deyneka at the Winona Lake Bible Conference. It lasted many hours and Brother Deyneka prayed several times, but seldom did a prayer of his last more than two minutes. His method was, "I send telegrams to heaven."

Someone has said, "*Length* in prayer often militates against *strength* in prayer."

Long prayers are fine—in private. When we are in meetings with others, our prayers should usually be short. Most prayers in the Bible are brief, to the point. The longest prayer recorded in Scripture is King Solomon's prayer delivered at the dedication of the Temple. It lasted about five minutes. All other biblical prayers are much shorter.

This story is told of D. L. Moody. In one of his meetings a brother continued to pray on and on and on. Moody became perturbed. Finally he called out, "While our brother is finishing his prayer, let us all sing hymn 276."

Was that discourteous, rude, and brusque? Maybe.

But here's another part of the story. A medical student was present on that occasion. During the long prayer this student became so bored that he reached for his hat and was ready to leave. But when Moody got them singing, the young man decided to remain. At the close, he was among those who came forward to receive Christ as Savior.

And that isn't all. That same young man later dedicated his life to missionary service and became one of the best known missionaries of his generation—Sir Wilfred Grenfell, medical missionary to Newfoundland.

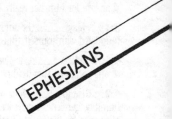
EPHESIANS

1:3 May today be a day of praise for _____ . May he/she give you glory for your countless blessings.

1:4 Lord, you chose us to be your children even before the foundation of the world. Your plan is that we should be holy. Give _____ both the desire and the power to live a holy life.

1:15, 16 As I think of _____'s faith in the Lord Jesus, and his/her love for other Christians, I want to give thanks to you for him/her.

1:17 Give to _____ wisdom, knowledge, and understanding.

2:10 Lord, we are your workmanship. We have been created for the purpose of doing good works/helping others. May this be fulfilled in the life of _____ .

3:12 Thank you, Lord, for the privilege of access into your presence. May _____ confidently take advantage of this high privilege.

3:16 May _____ be greatly strengthened and reinforced with mighty power. This power we know comes from the Holy Spirit.

3:17, 18 May _____ be rooted and grounded in love and able to comprehend (at least partially) how long . . . how wide . . . how deep . . . and how high your love for him/her really is.

3:19 May _____ be simply flooded with God . . . inundated with yourself (filled with all your fullness).

4:1, 2 Help _____ to live and act in a way worthy of our vocation. May his/her life be a credit to you.

4:2 Give to _____ four wonderful characteristics: humility, gentleness, patience, and forbearance (making allowance for the faults of others).

4:13, 14 Help _____ to put off childishness and put on maturity (be full-grown in the Lord).

4:13, 14 Give _____ victory over instability and gullibility. This will be achieved as his/her knowledge of God increases.

4:15 May _____ become more and more like you, Lord. You are the Head of the body of believers (the church). Help him/her to speak truly and live truly.

4:16 Lord, your plan is that Christians be joined and knit together, so that the whole body of Christ is healthy and full of love. May _____ help bring this pattern into glorious reality.

4:18, 13 Instead of a darkened understanding, may _____'s mind be filled with a knowledge of the Son of God.

4:18, 32 Instead of a blinded, insensitive, hardened heart, give to _____ a tender, enlightened, forgiving heart.

4:19, 24 Give _____ the power to "put off" sensuality, vice and uncleanness, and put on true holiness.

4:19, 28 Enable _____ to put off greed and put on generosity.

4:22, 24 Strengthen _____ to put off the old, evil nature which is rotten through and through and to put on the "new man" . . . be clothed with this new nature that is holy and good.

4:25 Help _____ to "put off" lying and "put on" truth.

4:26 Enable _____ to "put off" anger. May he/she not let the sun go down upon any wrath or loss of temper.

4:28 May _____ "put off" stealing, and "put on" honest labor.

4:29 May _____ "put off" bad language and corrupt communication—filthy speech. May his/her tongue be used to edify others, for that which is a blessing to other people.

4:30 Spare _____ from grieving the Holy Spirit in any way.

4:31, 32 Enable _____ to "put off" bitterness and "put on" kindness to others.

4:31, 32 Help _____ to "put off" being bad tempered and "put on" being tenderhearted.

4:31, 32 Give _____ power to "put off" quarreling —harsh words and hateful feelings—and "put on" a forgiving spirit.

5:2 Enable _____ to "put off" bitterness and resentments . . . and "put on" walking in love.

5:3 May there not be even a hint of sexual impurity in the life of _____ .

5:4 Lord, a good sense of humor is a blessing, but filthy jokes are a curse. Enable _____ to "put off" all such filthiness and foul talk and to "put on" giving of thanks.

5:5 Lord, we are not sinless, but help _____ to sin less and less.

5:7 Guide _____ in his/her choice of friends. May there be no partnership or close relationship with those who disobey you.

5:8, 9 Help _____ to "put off" darkness and walk as a child of light with three characteristics: goodness, righteousness, and truth.

5:10, 11 May _____ frequently ask the question, "Is this acceptable to you, Lord?" May he/she "put off" all that is not acceptable to you.

5:16 Lord, we fail in a multitude of ways, but one of our greatest failures is the foolish way we use our time. Help _____ to budget his/her time wisely so that he/she will not fritter away priceless moments and hours.

5:18 Lord, to "be filled with the Spirit" isn't just for a few . . . it is a command for all Christians. May _____ have a new filling of the Holy Spirit today.

5:19, 20 May _____ sing and make music in his/her heart to the Lord; always giving thanks to you for *everything*.

5:22 (For wives.) Help _____ to respect her husband and submit to him in like manner as she submits to you.

5:25 (For husbands.) Help _____ to love his wife in the same way that you love us.

6:1 (For sons and daughters.) Help _____ to obey his/her parents in the Lord, for this is right. May he/she honor and esteem his/her father and mother.

6:4 (For dads.) Help _____ to train and teach his children in the nurture and admonition of the Lord. Enable him to do this without provoking them to anger.

May he be deeply concerned about the salvation and
spiritual growth of his children.

6:10 May _____ learn to lean on you . . .
depending on your strength. May he/she be strong in
your almighty power.

6:11 Give _____ power to stand firmly against all
the wiles, schemes, and techniques of the devil.

6:13 Enable _____ to stand confidently on a
platform of faith—faith in your power.

6:16 Give _____ spiritual power as he/she battles
Satan . . . quenching all the fiery darts of the wicked.
May he/she use the shield of faith to resist the devil.

6:18 May _____ be a prayer warrior . . . continually in prayer, praying in the Spirit. Help him/her to
be alert and persevering.

Turn on the Praise Faucet!

Try this sometime. Before you start talking with the Lord, check your watch. Then close your eyes and don't ask the Lord for anything. Just thank him . . . praise him . . . worship him . . . thrill in his fellowship. As soon as you make a petition of some sort, open your eyes to see how much time has elapsed.

With most Christians it will be difficult to talk to God even one or two minutes without saying, "O Lord, give me _____ ." We are simply accustomed to making prayer a time of asking.

Now there is nothing wrong in making requests of God. In fact he greatly encourages us to, "Ask and it shall be given you." "Call unto me and I will answer thee." "Let your requests be made known unto God."

77

But frankly, prayer is so much more enjoyable—it is so much more fun—when we learn to spend time in praising, rather than petitioning.

Philippians stresses "turning on the praise faucet." (Prove it by reading 1:3; 4:4, 6.) This is the epistle of joy. The word "rejoice" appears ten times in these four chapters.

Here's something else you may want to try. Make a list of the people who have been the most encouraging to you in your life. Start with your childhood and on until the present (my list includes over a hundred such individuals). Then spend time simply saying "Thank you" to the Lord for them. It will be a unique blessing to you. "Turn on the praise faucet!"

1:3, 4 Lord, as I pray for _____ , my heart is full of joy. I thank you upon every remembrance of him/her.

1:5 As I mention the name of _____ I simply want to praise you for the fellowship in the gospel you have given me through him/her.

1:6 Lord, I am confident of this very thing—that you have begun a good work in _____ and that you will continue and perfect that work until the day of Jesus Christ. For this I sincerely thank you.

1:7-9 Lord, I have _____ in my heart. He/she shares your grace with me. I long after him/her that his/her love for you and for others may abound more and more this week.

1:10 I pray that _____ may approve things that are excellent and that he/she may be sincere and inwardly clean until the day of Christ.

1:20 Help _____ to always be ready to speak out boldly for Christ. I pray that the Lord Jesus might be magnified in his/her body . . . in health or in sickness, . . . by life or even by death.

1:26 I pray for _____ that his/her rejoicing in Christ might be more abundant this week than ever before.

1:27 May _____ conduct himself/herself this week in a manner worthy of the gospel of Christ. May he/she stand firm in one spirit with other Christians to strive unitedly for the spread of the gospel.

1:28, 29 Lord, I do not pray that _____ will be spared conflict or suffering, for unto us it is given, not only to believe, but also to suffer for the Lord's sake. I do pray that he/she will have a greater trust in you and may he/she "in nothing be terrified by adversaries or adversity."

2:1 Pour out upon _____ the consolation that is in Christ; the fellowship of the Holy Spirit; plus tenderness and compassion.

2:2 I pray for all in our congregation that they will love each other and work together with one heart, mind, and purpose. I pray this especially for _____ .

2:3 Help _____ to do nothing out of selfish ambition or vain conceit, but in lowliness of mind, let him/her esteem others better than himself/herself.

2:4-7 Help _____ not to look on his/her own interests but to be concerned about the interests of others. Exhort him/her to imitate the humility of the Lord Jesus. Eliminate from his/her life all graspiness and striving for reputation.

2:14 Teach _____ to do all things without murmuring, arguing, or fault-finding.

2:15, 16 In this crooked and perverse generation, help _____ to shine like a star in the heavens . . . clean, pure, and without fault, holding out to the unsaved the Word of life.

3:7 May the things that _____ used to consider gain now be loss to him/her . . . something to throw away, so that he/she can put his/her trust in Christ alone.

3:8 Enable _____ to count everything else as worthless compared with the gain of knowing Christ. May he/she be ready to lose everything and consider it all as mere rubbish in order to gain Christ.

3:10 Lord Jesus, I pray that _____ may really *know you* and the power of your resurrection and the fellowship of sharing in your sufferings.

3:13, 14 Instruct _____ to forget those things that are behind and reach forth unto those things which are before, to press toward the mark for the prize of the high calling of God in Christ Jesus.

4:1, 4 Help _____ to stand firm in the Lord and to rejoice in the Lord *all the time*.

4:5 May everyone be able to see in _____ unselfishness and consideration in all that he/she does. Help him/her to remember that the Lord is coming soon.

4:6 Give _____ the victory over worry, not being anxious about anything.

4:6, 7 Teach _____ that when we pray with thanksgiving, we will experience your peace, which is far more wonderful than the human mind can understand.

4:8 My prayer for _____ today is that he/she will fill his/her mind with things that are true . . . honest . . . just . . . pure . . . lovely . . . of good report.

4:11 Help _____ to be content today . . . whatever the circumstances might be.

4:12 As it was in the life of Paul, may it be similar in _____'s life, namely contentment in any circumstance whether he/she be abased or abound . . . whether he/she be in need or have plenty.

4:13 Help _____ to realize that he/she can do all things through Christ who strengthens him/her. May he/she seek your power for his/her needs today.

4:18   Help _____ to be faithful in giving financially to the work of the Lord, realizing that each gift is a sweet smelling sacrifice, well pleasing to you.

4:19, 23   O God, supply all of _____'s needs according to your glorious riches, and may your limitless grace be with him/her today . . . and every day.

**Pray
While
Driving**

One of the finest opportunities available for prayer is: while driving in your car. Especially if you are all alone.

Why waste those precious moments or hours? Of course you can listen to your car radio, but a far better plan is to talk to the Lord. Obviously this is another circumstance when you should pray with your eyes open! After all, the Bible tells us to "watch and pray"!

If I am on an expressway and there isn't much traffic, I love to pray and praise, especially the latter. One day while traveling from Lansing to Grand Rapids, I decided to simply praise the Lord for as many items as I could think of and not ask him for anything.

I thanked him for our "Savage" family (there are quite a few) . . . then for the people in our church (mentioning by name the deacons, the trustees, the Sunday school teachers, the choir members, the Awana leaders, the teens, the college age folk). Then I praised him for everyone I could think of who during my entire life has been of special encouragement to me. I gave thanks to the Lord for my car, for the good highway, for the beauty of nature along I-96, for my health, our government, etc. Believe it or not—I was still thanking him when I got to Grand Rapids! It was one of the most enjoyable times of prayer I've ever experienced. Try it sometime!

1:3, 4 I want to thank you for _____ . . . for his/her faith in Christ and his/her love for other Christians.

1:9 Help _____ to understand what you want him/her to do, and may he/she be wise concerning spiritual things.

1:10 May _____ live in a way that pleases you and honors you. May he/she continually do good and learn to know you better every day.

1:11 May _____ be filled with your mighty, glorious strength and keep going on with the Lord no matter what happens . . . always full of the joy of the Lord.

1:18 May you have the PREEMINENCE . . . the first place in the life of _____ .

1:23 Instruct _____ how to stand firm and steadfast in the faith. May he/she be strong in the Lord . . . unmoved by anyone or anything that would pull him/her away from the gospel.

1:28 Help _____ to talk about Christ to all who will listen . . . warning them and instructing them concerning their relationship with you.

2:2 May _____ be greatly encouraged today and knit together in love with other believers.

2:4 Lord, _____ needs protection from being deceived by smooth talk and enticing words. Please provide this protection for him/her.

2:7 Give _____ roots of faith that are firm and deep. May he/she be strong and vigorous in the truth . . . abounding with joy and thanksgiving.

2:8 Keep _____ from being swayed by vain deceit and deceptive philosophy . . . which are based on men's thoughts, instead of on what Christ taught us.

2:19 Lord, you are the head to which all of us are joined. Since _____ is a member of your body, may he/she grow wonderfully, receiving the nourishment and strength that you make available to us.

3:1, 2 _____ needs to seek those things which are above . . . to set his/her affections on things ABOVE, not on things of the earth. Give him/her the power to do this.

3:5 May _____ have nothing to do with sexual sin, impurity, lust, and shameful desires. Enable him/her to throw away all the rotten garments of anger, hatred, cursing, and dirty language.

3:9 Cleanse _____ from all lying and deceit.

3:10 May _____ learn more and more about what is right and what is wrong. May he/she be more and more like Jesus . . . renewed according to his image.

3:12 Help _____ to practice tenderhearted mercy and kindness to others and be ready to suffer quietly and patiently.

3:13 May _____ be ready to forgive. May he/she never hold grudges. Teach _____ that since you have forgiven him/her, he/she must forgive others.

3:15 May your peace rule in the heart of _____ and may he/she always be thankful.

3:16a May the teachings of the Lord Jesus dominate
_____'s life . . . that way he/she will have true
wisdom.

3:16b May _____ be inspired to sing to you with a
thankful heart; may he/she use the songs and Psalms to
edify and admonish others.

3:17 Whatever _____ does in word or deed, may
he/she do it all in the name of the Lord Jesus and give
you thanks.

3:18 (For wives.) Lord, this verse tells us that it is
right and fitting for wives to submit to their husbands.
Teach this to _____ .

3:19 (For husbands.) Lord, this verse tells us that
husbands should love their wives and not be harsh or
bitter with them. May this be true with _____ .

3:20 (For children.) This verse tells us it is well
pleasing to you when children obey their parents in all
things. May such be the pattern for _____ .

3:21 (For dads.) Help _____ to be a good dad, one
who is a great encouragement to his children. Show
him that they will become discouraged if he scolds them
excessively.

3:22 (For employees.) Help _____ to be an
exemplary employee, doing his/her work well because of
his/her love for the Lord. Help him/her to work cheerfully, as though working for you and not merely for the
boss.

4:1 (For employers.) Help _____ to be just and fair
to his/her employees, remembering he/she has a "boss"
in heaven.

4:2 May _____ be a faithful prayer warrior . . .
keeping at it, watching for your answers and then
remembering to be thankful for those answers to prayer.

4:5 Enable _____ to make the most of his/her chances to tell others about the gospel. Give him/her wisdom in dealing with the unsaved.

4:6 Give to _____ a gracious, sensible manner in speaking with others. May he/she know how to answer everyone.

4:12 Make _____ complete and perfect. Instruct him/her to know what your will is for him/her.

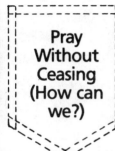

Pray Without Ceasing (How can we?)

In order to pray, do we have to be talking? If so,—then to "pray without ceasing" (1 Thessalonians 5:17) is an impossibility. No one can talk to the Lord twenty-four hours every day.

My favorite definition of prayer is: "practicing the presence of Jesus." Prayer is recognizing that the Lord is seated (or standing) right beside us . . . *all the time*, and having fellowship with him at all hours.

When my wife and I drive somewhere she is right beside me. I am in fellowship with her. Do we talk all the time? No way! But I am "practicing the presence of Wilda." She is "practicing the presence of Bob." And we do that "without ceasing."

That's the way prayer should be. We "practice the presence of the Lord" and we do it "without ceasing." Often we talk . . . often we are silent. Sometimes we ask him for things . . . more frequently we simply want to tell him how grateful we are for his blessings.

Warren Wiersbe admonishes us never to say, "Lord, we come into thy presence." We should be in his presence *all the time*. We should never leave his presence!

1:3 Lord, as _____ looks forward to the coming of Christ, give him/her strong faith, love, and patience.

1:9 Help _____ to turn completely from any idol in his/her heart and give first place to you—the living and true God.

1:10 The believers in Thessalonica were looking forward to your return from heaven. May this be true of _____ . May he/she live in such a way that your coming will bring him/her great joy.

2:6 Give _____ victory over seeking the praise of people.

3:2, 3 May _____ be established, encouraged, and comforted in the faith . . . and not become upset, dismayed, or fainthearted because of afflictions.

4:3, 4 May _____ be characterized by purity and honor . . . especially in sexual matters.

4:7 O Lord, you have not called us to lust, but to be holy and clean. May _____ be molded by you to conform to this calling.

4:11 May _____ seek to live a quiet life, minding his/her own business and diligently working at his/her job.

5:5, 6 O Lord, _____ does not belong to darkness and night . . . he/she is a child of the light. So help him/her to be awake, alert and serving you, waiting and watching for your return.

5:11 Make _____ an apostle of encouragement to other Christians. May he/she edify others and build them up.

5:12, 13 May _____ give the leaders of the church his/her wholehearted love and esteem.

5:13 O Lord, emancipate _____ from all quarreling.

5:14 Help _____ to warn those who are lazy; to comfort those who are timid; to care for those who are weak (spiritually and physically); to be patient with everyone.

5:15 Lord, give _____ victory over vindictiveness . . . rendering evil for evil. Help him/her to seek ways of doing good to everyone.

5:16 Help _____ to rejoice at all times.

5:18 Give _____ the ability to give thanks in everything, for this is your will for all of us.

5:19 Purify _____ so that he/she will not quench the Holy Spirit.

5:20 Help _____ not to neglect Bible study.

5:21 Lord, enable _____ to test and examine all things to be sure they are true . . . and whatever is true, help him/her to hold fast to it.

5:22 Give _____ the desire and power to abstain from all appearance of evil.

5:23 Make _____ entirely clean. May his/her spirit, soul, and body be kept strong and blameless until the return of our Lord.

Arrows from the Quiver of Prayer

Talking to men about God is great—but talking to God about men is greater.

When praying, do not give God instructions—simply report for duty!

Prayer is not overcoming God's reluctance—it is laying hold of his highest willingness.

You cannot stumble if you are on your knees.

The best citizens in our nation are the parents who teach their children how to pray.

Motto in a church: "If you must whisper, whisper a prayer."

If your knees knock, kneel on them.

A child once prayed, "O Lord, make the bad people good, and the good people nice."

Another child prayed, "O Lord, please also take care of yourself. We'd be in an awful fix if anything should happen to you."

93

1:5 Give to _____ a pure heart, a clean mind, and a strong faith.

1:6 Spare _____ from jangling, purposeless arguing and foolish talk.

1:17 May a spirit of worship inundate _____ . May he/she exalt you as the King eternal, immortal, invisible, the only wise God . . . giving you all honor and glory forever and ever.

1:18, 19 May _____ be a valiant fighter in this warfare against sin and Satan, clinging tightly to his/her faith in Christ, keeping his/her conscience clear, doing what he/she knows is right.

2:1, 2 Help _____ to pray much for all people and do it with thanksgiving. Lay it on his/her heart to intercede for all who are in authority over us or are in places of high responsibility.

2:8 Cleanse _____ from anger, quarreling, and resentment.

2:9, 10 (For women.) May _____ choose modest clothing. May she be good, kind, and sensible and not be known for her jewelry, expensive clothes, and elaborate hairstyles.

3:2 (For pastors and church leaders.) May _____ be above reproach . . . vigilant, hard working, thoughtful, orderly, and a good Bible teacher.

3:3 Help _____ to be gentle, patient, and kind. Free him/her from the love of money, wine, and quarreling.

3:8, 9 May _____ not be a lover of money or wine. Help him/her to be sincere in all he/she says, an earnest, wholehearted follower of Christ, with a clear conscience.

4:7, 8 I pray that _____ will not waste his/her time arguing over silly ideas and foolish doctrines. Help him/her to give priority to the exercise of keeping spiritually fit.

4:12 (For young men.) Enable _____ to be an example to all believers of every age bracket . . . a pattern for them in his speech, his conduct, his love, faith, and purity.

4:13 (For pastors, teachers.) Help _____ to be a diligent reader and to explain clearly the Scriptures . . . preaching the Word and teaching sound doctrine.

4:14, 15 Lord, _____ has special abilities you have given him/her. May he/she put these abilities to work so that his/her progress will be evident to everyone.

4:16 Help _____ to persevere and keep a close watch on all he/she does or thinks . . . always staying true and faithful to your will.

6:1, 2 (For employees.) May _____ be diligent at his/her place of employment. May it not be said that Christians are poor employees.

6:6, 10 May _____ combine godliness and contentment in his/her life . . . not greedy for lots of money. The love of money could cause him/her to yield to all kinds of evil temptations.

6:11 _____ is God's man/woman. Help him/her to follow after righteousness, godliness, faith, love, patience, and meekness.

6:12 Help _____ to fight the good fight of faith.

6:14 May _____ fulfill all you have told him/her to do . . . so that no one can find fault with him/her right up to the time the Lord returns.

6:17 May _____ not be proud or high-minded. May he/she not trust in fleeting riches, but rather trust totally in you, because you give us richly all we need.

6:18, 19 Help _____ to use his/her money to do good and be rich in good works . . . always ready to share with others in their needs. May he/she store up a treasure for himself/herself in *heaven* . . . that's the only safe investment for eternity.

More Arrows

Prayer for a football team: "Lord, if we win, keep us humble enough not to boast. If we lose, give us grace not to make excuses."

God grant me the serenity to accept things I cannot change, the courage to change things I can, and the wisdom to know the difference.

When you don't know what to do next— don't do it!

Do not face the day until you have faced God.

Prayer never was intended as a means to get the Lord to help us out of problems caused by our laziness.

Let us not rebel against delay. God's time will come. We must not steal tomorrow out of God's hands. God is never too late. He is always right on time.

People who do a lot of kneeling don't do much lying.

If the devil cannot beat you in prayer, he cannot beat you anywhere.

If you are too busy to pray, you are busier than God wants you to be.

1:6 May _____ get on fire for you, Lord. May he/she fan into flame the gift . . . the talent you have given him/her.

1:7 Lord, _____ needs victory over fear. Show him/her that you have not given us the spirit of fear, but rather the spirit of power, love, and discipline.

1:8 May _____ never be ashamed to tell others about our Lord.

1:9 Lord, you have saved us and called us to a *holy life*. May there be a consistent pattern of holiness in _____'s life.

1:12 _____ needs confidence and assurance. Enable him/her to say: "I know whom I have believed and I am persuaded that he is able to keep what I have committed to him."

1:13 Lord, help _____ to hold tight to the pattern of truth he/she hears at church each week. May _____ combine Bible doctrine and good works.

2:1 Lord, you want us to be strong spiritually . . . strong with the strength that comes from you. May _____ have this strength today and everyday.

2:2 May there be a chain reaction in our midst. For example, help _____ to pass on to others the lessons he/she has learned, and then may those people in turn share these great truths with still others.

2:3 Help _____ to be a good soldier of Jesus Christ and learn how to endure hardship.

2:5 In living the Christian life, enable _____ to be like a good athlete, recognizing that unless the rules are observed, no one can win the victor's crown. Help _____ to faithfully observe your rules.

2:14 Help _____ not to get into quarrels over unimportant trivia. Such arguments are confusing, useless, and even harmful.

2:15 I pray that _____ will study to show himself/herself approved unto God, a workman who does not need to be ashamed when you examine him/her. And help him/her to rightly interpret your Word.

2:16 Give _____ the ability to steer clear of godless chatter, foolish discussion, profane and vain babblings which quench fervor for the Lord and increase ungodliness.

2:19 O God, your truth stands firm like a rock and nothing can shake it. You know those who are yours. _____ belongs to you. Help him/her to depart from all sin and iniquity.

2:21 Enable _____ to stay away from sin and be like a dish of purest gold . . . made holy and useful to you for your highest and best assignments.

2:22 (For young people.) Help _____ to run from youthful lusts. May he/she have faith, love, and peace, and seek the companionship of those who love you and have pure hearts.

2:23 Protect _____ from foolish and senseless arguments, which only upset people and cause quarrels.

2:24, 25   Help _____ to be gentle and kind to everyone . . . courteously and patiently teaching those who are confused concerning the truth.

2:26   O Lord, the devil is seeking to ensnare _____ . Give him/her power to resist Satan and not be trapped by any of his diabolic schemes or techniques.

3:2   Emancipate _____ from being self-centered . . . and help him/her not to be a lover of money.

3:2   Give _____ victory over boasting, pride, disobedience to his/her parents.

3:4   May _____ not be a lover of pleasure, but rather a lover of God.

3:5   Lord, often we manifest a form of godliness, but we deny the power thereof. May such not be the case in _____'s life.

3:10   May _____ have the right combination of sound doctrine plus a way of life that honors you. What he/she believes should be in harmony with the way he/she lives.

3:13   I pray that _____ will not be deceived or led astray by evil men and false teachers.

3:14, 15   May _____ continue in the things he/she has learned. Develop in him/her a wisdom that is gained from the Holy Scriptures.

3:16   Teach _____ that all the Bible is given by divine inspiration. All Scripture is "God-breathed." May he/she study it diligently to know what is true and to realize what needs to be corrected in his/her life.

4:2   May _____ proclaim your Word to others today. May he/she have a sense of urgency to do this "in season and out of season" (whether the circumstances are favorable or unfavorable).

4:4 Lord, it's a temptation for all of us to turn our ears away from the truth and listen to ideas men have concocted. Give _____ power to overcome that temptation.

4:7 Help _____ to fight long and hard for the Lord; to finish the race; to keep the faith.

4:8 I pray that _____ may love your appearing . . . eagerly looking forward to your return.

4:18 O Lord, deliver _____ from every evil work. Preserve and keep him/her each step of the way until you bring us into the kingdom of heaven.

The Lines Are All Busy!

A Los Angeles newspaper carried the story about an attempted break-in. An elderly woman who lived alone heard some strange noises outside her window. Peeking through the curtain, she was horrified to see a man trying to pry his way in. Rushing to the phone, she frantically dialed the police headquarters. To her dismay she got the announcement, "I'm very sorry. The lines are all busy! Please call again—this is a recording." With increased anxiety, she made a second attempt, but again she heard the same discouraging words, "The lines are all busy."

We rejoice that the "royal telephone" which connects earth and heaven never has this problem. The lines are never busy. Our heavenly Father, the Governor of the universe, is never "too busy" when we want to call him.

Isaiah 65:24 assures us, "I will answer them before they even call to me. While they are still talking to me about their needs, I will go ahead and answer their prayers!"

Furthermore, this royal telephone is available to us—twenty-four hours a day.

Psalm 55:17 proves this. "I will pray morning, noon, and night, pleading aloud with God; and he will hear and answer."

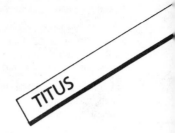

1:8 Help _____ to be hospitable, a lover of all that is good. May he/she be self-controlled, upright, holy, and disciplined.

1:9 May _____ hold fast the faithful truths he/she has been taught, so that he/she can encourage others by sound doctrine and refute those who oppose it.

2:2 May _____ be serious and unruffled, sensible, knowing and believing the truth, doing everything with love and patience.

2:5 (For wives.) Help _____ to be sensible, clean-minded, a good housekeeper, and obedient to her husband.

2:7 Give strength to _____ to be an example of good works and be characterized by integrity, seriousness, and sincerity.

2:8 May _____ be characterized by speech so sound, sensible, and logical that any who oppose him/her will be silenced and ashamed of themselves.

2:12 Give _____ power to say "no" to ungodliness and worldly lusts . . . to live a life that is self-controlled, upright, and godly.

2:13   May _____ be constantly looking for that blessed hope and the glorious appearing of our Savior Jesus Christ.

2:14   Rescue _____ from falling into sin. May he/she have a real enthusiasm to do what is good . . . and be purified unto the Lord.

3:1   Help _____ to obey the government and its officers, and always be obedient and ready for any honest work.

3:2   Encourage _____ not to speak evil of anyone, nor be quarrelsome, but gentle, showing courtesy to everybody.

3:3   Emancipate _____ from being foolish, disobedient, deceived, or enslaved by passions and pleasures.

3:8, 9   May _____ be devoted to doing good deeds. Enable him/her to avoid foolish controversies, arguments, and quarrels. These things are unprofitable and useless.

We
Are
Lazy

My esteemed Russian brother, Peter Deyneka, is known far and wide for his formula: Much prayer —much power; Little prayer—little power; No prayer—no power.

And we all recognize that. We nod our heads in agreement. Yet we do not pray with the fervency and frequency we ought. Why is this?

Jesus gave us the answer . . . in Matthew 26:41. "Keep alert and pray. Otherwise temptation will overpower you. For the spirit indeed is willing, but how weak [and lazy] the body is!"

There you have it! We know we ought to pray more. We frequently resolve we will. The "spirit is willing." But unfortunately the "flesh is weak."

Most of us are lazy . . . and prayer is *work*. The flesh isn't too anxious to work.

The reason many don't attend the prayer meetings of their church is—they are *lazy*.

2:1 May _____ listen very carefully to the truths he/she has heard (concerning your Word) and in this way keep from drifting away.

2:3 (For the unsaved.) What makes _____ think he/she can escape if he/she is indifferent to this great salvation? Instead of continuing in indifference, I pray that he/she may soon make a definite decision to trust Christ.

2:18 Lord, you know what it is to go through the same temptations we face. May _____ realize this and lean on you, seeking your help in every temptation or trial he/she has.

3:6 Enable _____ to keep up his/her courage, firm to the end, along with joy and trust in the Lord.

3:7, 8 The people of Israel complained and murmured when you tested them in the desert. Emancipate _____ from such grumbling. May he/she be careful to hear your voice today and keep his/her heart tender to you.

3:14 You have promised that if we are faithful to the end, trusting you just as we did when we first became Christians, that we will share in all that belongs to Christ. Give to _____ this kind of faithfulness.

3:15 (For the unsaved.) Help _____ to heed the warning, "Today if you hear God's voice speaking to you, do not harden your heart, as the people of Israel did when they rebelled against him in the desert."

4:12 Thank you, Lord, for the Bible. It is full of living power. It is sharper than the sharpest dagger, cutting swiftly and deeply into our innermost thoughts . . . exposing us for what we really are. May _____ recognize this and have a great appetite to feed on your Word.

4:13 Lord, everything about us is bare and wide open to your all-seeing eyes. Nothing can be hidden from you. May this truth be impressed upon _____ and produce in him/her a pattern of life that is pleasing to you.

4:16 May _____ be a man/woman of prayer . . . approaching the throne of grace with confidence, to find your strength to help in every need he/she has this week.

5:14 Help _____ to feed on solid spiritual food . . . and in this way train himself/herself to distinguish good from evil.

6:1 Help _____ to advance beyond the kindergarten teachings about Christ and go on to spiritual maturity.

6:12 Give _____ the victory over laziness. Help him/her to imitate men and women of faith and patience.

10:22 Since (by the blood of Jesus) we can have confidence to enter into your holy presence, help _____ to draw near to you with a sincere heart . . . in full assurance of faith.

10:25 May _____ spur other Christians on toward love and good deeds.

10:25 Help _____ not to forsake or neglect the church services (as some are doing). May he/she encourage and edify others.

10:36 Help _____ to persevere . . . knowing that by submitting to your will, he/she will receive what you have promised.

11:6 May _____ please you by having great faith . . . because without faith it is impossible to please you.

11:8 May _____ have such faith in you, that he/she will be ready to go anywhere you indicate for him/her.

11:10 May _____ live with eternity's values in view . . . looking forward to the city whose architect and builder is God.

11:26 May _____ regard following Jesus as of greater value than the so-called treasures of this world. May he/she look beyond this world for his/her reward.

12:1 May _____ throw off everything that hinders him/her in following you. May he/she have victory over the sin that so easily besets him/her.

12:1 May _____ run with patience and perseverance the race you have marked out for him/her.

12:2 May _____ not have his/her eyes fixed on people, but rather on you, Lord. You are the Author and Finisher of our faith.

12:3 Help _____ not to grow weary and lose heart.

12:5, 6 Give _____ the right attitude about your chastening. May he/she not become disheartened when you reprove him/her . . . because we know you chasten those whom you love.

12:10 Lord, we know that you discipline us for our good . . . that we may share your holiness. So help _____ to submit to you 100 percent—and to your chastening and discipline.

12:14, 15 May _____ not have any bitterness toward anyone. May he/she live in peace with everybody and be holy.

12:16 Give _____ victory over sexual immorality and any other form of godlessness.

12:28 May _____ be thankful and worship you with deep reverence.

13:4 May _____'s marriage be kept pure . . . free from adultery and all that is immoral.

13:5 Emancipate _____ from the love of money and may he/she be content with what he/she has.

13:9 Help _____ to not be carried away by any kind of strange teachings. May his/her heart be strengthened by your grace.

13:15 May _____ continually offer you a sacrifice of praise; not forgetting to do good and to share with others.

But I Can't Pray in Public

Question: Why is it that many people are afraid to pray in public?

Answer: Because they are concerned about what people will think of their prayers. They are afraid that their prayers will not sound as beautiful as another person's prayer.

So we need to ask ourselves, "Who am I trying to impress with my prayer—other people or God?"

A newspaper reported a civic ceremony with the words, "The Reverend Doctor Archibald McKinney directed a beautiful prayer to those assembled."

That's where many public prayers are directed—to the people, rather than to God. And probably God isn't very much impressed.

If we are unconcerned about people and

only concerned about communicating with God, then it really isn't important if we must hesitate and hunt for words. The Lord isn't swayed by beautiful phrases and pious-sounding words. He is interested in the condition of our hearts. If we exhibit worship, sincerity, helplessness, and faith in our praying, we are "getting through" to God, whether or not we have a rich vocabulary.

JAMES

1:2, 3 May _____ count it all joy when he/she faces testing and temptation . . . knowing that the testing of our faith is good for us. It produces patience.

1:4 Help _____ to let patience have its perfect work in his/her heart . . . so that he/she may become mature and complete.

1:19 May _____ be quick to listen . . . slow to speak and slow to become angry.

1:21 Give _____ victory over the moral filth that is so prevalent and may he/she welcome your Word which has been planted in his/her heart.

1:22 May _____ be a doer of your Word, and not a hearer only.

3:17 Give _____ wisdom from above that is pure and peaceable.

3:17 Give _____ wisdom from above that is gentle and easy to be entreated.

3:17 Give _____ wisdom from above that is full of mercy and good fruit.

3:17 Give _____ wisdom from above that is without partiality and without hypocrisy.

4:7 Give _____ the power to resist the devil so vigorously that Satan will flee from him/her.

4:8 Help _____ to draw near to you . . . and to cleanse his/her hands and purify his/her heart.

4:11 Help _____ not to speak evil about other Christians. When we do that we fight against your law, which commands us to love one another.

5:7, 8 Help _____ to be patient . . . waiting for the Lord's coming. Help him/her to stand firm because your return is near.

5:9 Help _____ not to grumble against others.

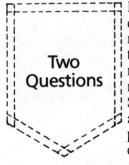

Two Questions

First: Would you choose to be a member of a church that doesn't have a mid-week prayer meeting?
Second: Do you attend the mid-week prayer service of your church?

1:7 May _____'s faith be proved genuine and result in your praise, honor, and glory.

1:8 Fill _____ with a joy unspeakable (too great for words) and full of glory.

1:13 Exhort _____ to get in "on the action"; to be self-controlled and have his/her hope set on the grace to be revealed when Christ returns.

1:14 May _____ be obedient to you and not conform to the evil desires he/she had formerly.

1:15 May _____ be holy in all that he/she does . . . in all his/her conduct and manner of living.

1:17 Teach _____ that you have no favorites . . . that you will judge with perfect justice everything we do. Then help _____ to conduct himself/herself with reverence during this earthly pilgrimage.

1:22 Help _____ to deeply love the others in the family of God with a pure and fervent heart.

2:1 Give _____ the power to rid himself/herself of all malice, deceit, hypocrisy, envy, and slander.

2:2 Give to _____ a big appetite for the pure milk of the Word. May there be a wonderful spiritual growth in his/her life.

2:11 Enable _____ to abstain from physical lust and passions which war against the soul.

2:12 May _____ live such a good life before the unsaved, that though they may criticize him/her, they will see his/her good deeds and glorify the Lord.

2:13 May _____ learn how to submit to every authority.

2:16 Teach _____ the meaning of freedom. It isn't doing our own thing; it isn't following any or every desire. But freedom is emancipation from serving sin, plus the opportunity and privilege of serving you.

2:17 May _____ show respect for everybody. May he/she love the brothers and sisters in Christ. May he/she fear you.

3:1, 2 (For wives.) May _____ be submissive to her husband. May she gain his admiration with purity and godliness.

3:3, 4 (For women.) May _____ be beautiful . . . not with outward adornment, but with an inner beauty —the unfading beauty of a gentle and quiet spirit.

3:7 (For husbands.) May _____ be considerate and thoughtful of his wife and her needs, and honor her as a weaker partner. May he remember that if he doesn't treat her as he should, his prayers will be hindered.

3:8 Christians should be like one big, happy family . . . full of sympathy toward each other and loving one another with tender hearts and humble minds. May this be characteristic of _____ .

3:9 May _____ not be vindictive (repaying evil with evil). Rather may he/she repay evil with blessing.

3:10 Give to _____ the ability to control his/her tongue and cleanse his/her lips of deceit.

3:11 Help _____ to turn away from all evil. May he/she try to live in peace even if he/she must run after it to catch it.

3:14, 15 Help _____ not to be afraid or troubled. Enable him/her to quietly trust you. If anyone asks him/her about his/her Christian faith, may he/she be prepared to answer in a gentle and respectful way.

3:16 Help _____ to do what is right. Then if others speak against him/her, they will become ashamed of themselves because of their false accusations.

3:17 When and if _____ is called upon to go through trials and suffering, help him/her to realize it is better to suffer for doing good than for doing wrong.

4:2 Help _____ to be anxious to do your will and not chase after evil desires.

4:4, 5 Encourage _____ if his/her former friends laugh at him/her because of his/her Christian standards. Help him/her to realize that they must face the Judge and that they will be punished for the way they live.

4:7 Lord, the end of the world is coming soon, so help _____ to be an earnest, thoughtful man/woman of prayer.

4:8 May _____ continue to show a deep love for other Christians. Love overlooks others' many faults.

4:9 (For couples.) Give to _____ the spirit of hospitality . . . cheerfully sharing their home with those who need a meal or a place to stay for the night.

4:10 Lord, you have given each of us some special abilities. Help _____ to use his/her talents in service to others.

4:11 Bestow upon _____ the gift of helping others, and may he/she do it with the strength and energy you supply, so that you will be glorified in it all.

4:12, 13 May _____ not be surprised or bewildered when and if trials come. Instead may he/she be really glad—because these trials will make him/her a partner with Christ in his suffering and eligible to share his glory.

5:2, 3 (For pastors.) Help _____ to feed the flock of believers placed under his care. May he oversee the flock . . . and may he be an example to the flock.

5:5 (For young men.) Help _____ to follow the leadership of those who are older.

5:5 Lord, your Word instructs us that we are to serve each other with humble spirits; and that you give special blessings to those who are humble, but set yourself against those who are proud. May _____ be clothed with genuine humility.

5:7 May _____ learn to cast all his/her care upon you . . . confident that you are caring for us.

5:8 May _____ be careful and vigilant, knowing that our adversary, the devil, is prowling around like a hungry, roaring lion, seeking whom he may devour.

5:9 Help _____ to firmly resist Satan, realizing that other Christians all around the world are also going through trials and suffering.

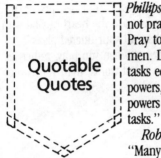

Quotable Quotes

Phillips Brooks: "Do not pray for easy lives. Pray to be stronger men. Do not pray for tasks equal to your powers, but pray for powers equal to your tasks."

Robert A. Cook: "Many of us close the door to the Almighty's working in our lives because we neglect to praise God when we pray. Praise opens the door of faith. Praise lets me abandon myself to God just as I am. Praise lets my spirit fly out of the cage of unbelief. Praise in the present tense assures future victory."

A. W. Tozer: "Selfishness is never so exquisitely selfish as when it is on its knees. Self turns what would otherwise be a pure and powerful prayer into a weak and ineffective one. I may cry loudly to God that the church be restored to her New Testament splendor, and secretly dream that *I* may be the one to lead her.''

Martin Luther: "I have so much to do I must needs pray two hours a day."

St. Augustine: "O Lord, grant that I may do *Thy* will as if it were *my* will, so that Thou mayest do *my* will as if it were *Thy* will."

O. Hallesby: "Prayer and helplessness are inseparable. Only he who is helpless can truly pray. Your helplessness is your best prayer. It calls from your heart to the heart of God with greater effect than all your uttered pleas."

John Bunyan: "When you pray, rather let your heart be without words, than your words without heart."

1:5 Empower _____ to add to his/her faith . . . virtue, courage, and knowledge.

1:6 May _____ add to his/her faith . . . self-control, patience, and godliness.

1:7 May _____ add to his/her faith . . . brotherly kindness and love.

2:10 Help _____ *not* to follow the corrupt desires of sinful nature, nor to despise authority.

2:18 Help _____ *not* to mouth empty, boastful words, nor yield to the lustful desires of sinful, human nature.

3:8, 9 Encourage _____ to wait upon you, recognizing that with you one day is as a thousand years and a thousand years are as a day; that you are not slow in keeping your promises, but are patient with us.

3:11, 13 Empower _____ to live a holy and godly life as he/she looks forward to the day of the Lord . . . and to a new heaven and new earth.

3:14 As _____ anticipates the Second Coming, may he/she make every effort to be spotless, blameless, and at peace with you.

3:18 Enable _____ this week to grow in grace and in the knowledge of our Lord and Savior Jesus Christ.

Definitions of Prayer

Prayer is pulling the switch that operates the powerhouse of heaven.

Prayer is the sincerest desire of the soul, expressed heavenward.

Prayer is the sweet incense rising from a broken heart.

Prayer is practicing the presence of Jesus.

Prayer is the expression of the human heart in conversation with God (Rosalind Rinker).

Prayer is a dialogue between two persons who love each other (Rosalind Rinker).

Prayer is the powerhouse of the church.

Prayer is the highest skill of the spirit. It is a consuming passion, the very life and breath of Christian living.

Prayer is weakness leaning on omnipotence (W. S. Bowden).

Prayer is quietly opening a door and slipping into the very presence of God.

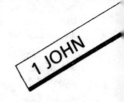

1:4   May _____ be filled with the joy of the Lord today.

1:7   Give to _____ friendship and fellowship with other Christians. Help him/her to realize that to "have fellowship one with another" we should walk in the light.

1:9   Motivate _____ to quickly and sincerely confess any and every sin he/she commits, assured that you will immediately forgive that sin and cleanse him/her from all unrighteousness when confession is made.

2:1, 2   Enable _____ to stay away from sin. But if he/she sins, may he/she avail himself/herself of our Advocate (Mediator), namely you, blessed Lord, to obtain forgiveness for that sin.

2:5   Empower _____ to do what you tell him/her to do and to learn to love you more and more.

2:6   May _____'s standard of right and wrong be based upon following "in his steps," that is, walking in the way Jesus walked and asking: "What would Jesus do?"

2:15   Enable _____ to neither be conformed to the world nor to withdraw from it. You have commanded us not to love the world, but you have sent us into the world to be a witness to everybody.

2:16   Cleanse _____ from all worldly things . . . the craze for sex, the desire to obtain everything coveted by the lust of the eyes, and the pride of life. These are not from you, Lord, they are from this evil world.

2:17   Lord, this world is fading away, and lust will go with it, but whoever is faithful in doing your will abides forever. May _____ do exactly this.

2:21   Give _____ the ability to discern the difference between true and false.

2:24   Help _____ to keep on believing what he/she has been taught from the beginning. In this way he/she will maintain close fellowship with you.

2:27   Blessed Holy Spirit, you are the One who teaches us all things. Enable _____ to abide in you, leaning on you for guidance in everything.

2:28   May _____ abide in you, so that when you appear he/she will have confidence and not be ashamed before you at your coming.

3:1-3   Heavenly Father, we are amazed by how much you love us. You give us the title "Sons of God." When our Lord returns we shall be like him. All who really believe this, purify themselves. Help _____ to do exactly this.

3:6   Instruct _____ to stay close to you; obedient to you; not sinning. Those who keep sinning have never really known you.

3:9   The person born into your family, Father, does not habitually sin, because your life is in him. May there be no habitual sin in _____'s life.

3:17   May your love be evident in the life of _____ . May he/she have compassion for those with material needs.

3:24 Give to _____ the desire and strength to do what you tell him/her to do. This is the way you live in us and we live in you. We know this is true because the Holy Spirit tells us so.

4:1 Help _____ to not gullibly believe everything that certain people claim is a message from God. Instruct him/her to test every teaching first . . . whether it is really from you.

4:7, 11 May _____ be loving and kind, for this shows we are children (born of God) and that we know you.

4:17 May _____ grow more perfect and complete in his/her love for others. This will give him/her confidence in the day of judgment.

4:18 Give _____ victory over fear. We know that you love us perfectly. If we are afraid, it shows we do not fully trust you.

5:3 Show _____ that loving you means doing what you tell us to do, and really that isn't too difficult.

5:4 All of us who are born again have the power to overcome the world . . . and this is the victory that overcomes the world, even our faith. May _____ be that kind of overcomer.

5:13 Give to _____ a "know-so" confidence that he/she has eternal life.

5:14 Your Word assures us that you are listening if we pray for that which is in harmony with your will. Give to _____ this confidence.

5:21 Empower _____ to stay away from anything or anybody that might take God's place (the number one spot) in his/her heart.

I Wish
I Had
Your
Corn

The story is told of a farmer whose harvest of corn was unusually large. All the bins of his barns were full. He was a Christian and would often pray. He prayed for the poor and needy, "O God, I pray that their wants will be supplied."

One day an impoverished man who had several children asked the farmer for a bagful of corn, but the farmer said he didn't have any to spare.

The next morning the farmer's daughter heard him pray again for the poor and needy. She said to him, "Daddy, I wish I had your corn."

"Why do you say that?"

"If I had your corn, I'd use it to answer your prayers."

Many people pray, "O God, I pray that somehow my neighbor will have the plan of salvation explained to him." Well, why don't you simply go and rap on the door of your neighbor and do the explaining?

Others pray, "O Lord, so-and-so is lonely and needs some Christian friends and fellowship. Please provide her with this fellowship." Well, why don't you do what D. L. Moody used to suggest: "Put shoe leather to your prayers!"

3 May _____ earnestly contend for the faith . . . stoutly defending the truth you have given (which never changes).

16, 17 Enable _____ to remember what has been told us by the apostles. May he/she be apostolic in doctrine and practice.

16-19 May _____ not be influenced by the murmurers, complainers, and gripers who stir up arguments; who love the evil things of this world and who do not have the Holy Spirit living in them.

20 Motivate _____ to build up his/her life more strongly on the foundation of our holy faith; learning to pray in the power and strength of the Holy Spirit.

22 Grant _____ the ability to help those who are argumentative and to be merciful to those who have doubts.

23 May _____ be a soul-winner, snatching sinners from the very flames of hell itself.

23 Empower _____ to loathe even the garment that is polluted with sin. Instruct him/her to be merciful to sinners, but at the same time to hate every trace of their sin.

24 May praise fill the life of _____ , giving all glory to Jesus. Splendor, majesty, power, and authority are yours, Lord.

24 May a doxology fill the heart of _____ . May he/she rejoice that you are able to keep us from falling and bring us sinless and perfect into your presence with mighty shouts of everlasting joy. Amen!

You Be the Compiler!

I covet for you the same blessing I've received in culling from God's Word these 700+ ways of praying for others . . . and I'm delighted you are using the result of my personal study. But let me suggest that you compile your own collection! I guarantee this will be one of the most inspiring, blessed, and rewarding methods of Bible study you've ever followed!

Let me give you a few suggestions:

First, choose a book of the Bible, and as you study it ask the question, "What suggestions do I find in these chapters for prayer patterns?"

Second, underline the verses that contain suggestions of this sort.

Third, once you have a cluster of ideas, write them out as prayer or praise requests.

You can use the exact wording you find in

the Bible; or you can make a personal paraphrase of it; or you can compare several versions and combine them into the wording you personally prefer.

Fourth, when you have typed or written out twenty or more of these requests (personally compiled by you), then use these to pray for people you have on your personal prayer list.

I know you will be greatly blessed when you become your own compiler! Perhaps eventually *you* will produce a list of more than 700 ways to pray for others!

1:1 Help _____ not to walk in the counsel of the ungodly; nor follow the advice of evil men; nor hang around with sinners.

1:2 May _____ delight in doing what you want him/her to do, meditating day and night in your Word.

5:3 Make _____ a man/woman of prayer, looking to you each morning, laying his/her requests before you, praying earnestly.

5:7 May _____ worship you with deepest awe, and be protected by your mercy and your love.

5:11 Let all those who put their trust in you rejoice. May they keep shouting for joy because you defend them. May this be true of _____ .

6:2 (For those who are sick.) Have pity on _____ , for he/she is weak. Heal him/her, for his/her body is sick. He/she is upset and disturbed. His/her mind is filled with apprehension and gloom. O Lord, restore him/her soon.

7:9, 10 Lord, you look deep within our hearts. You examine all our motives and thoughts; you are our shield. I pray that you will defend _____ and establish him/her.

141

7:17   May _____ say with David, "Oh, how grateful and thankful I am to the Lord because he is so good. I will sing praise to the name of the Lord."

9:1, 2   May _____ praise you with all his/her heart, and tell everyone about the marvelous things you do. May he/she be glad, yes, filled with joy because of you, and may he/she sing your praises.

9:9, 10   Lord, all who are oppressed may come to you. All those who know your mercy count on you for help. This is the situation of _____ . Be a refuge for him/her in this time of trouble.

13:5, 6   May _____ always trust in you and in your mercy. May he/she rejoice in your salvation and sing to the Lord because you have blessed him/her so richly.

15:1-3   Lord, who can find refuge and shelter in your presence? The requirement is to walk uprightly, to speak the truth, not to slander others, not to listen to gossip, and not to harm his/her neighbors. May _____ fulfill this requirement.

15:4   Help _____ to speak out against sin and against those committing it. Also help him/her to encourage and commend the faithful followers of the Lord. May he/she always keep his/her promises even though they might cost him/her greatly.

16:5   May worship fill the heart of _____ , saying with David, "The Lord himself is my inheritance, my prize. He is my food and drink, my highest joy! He guards all that is mine."

16:8, 9   May _____ always be thinking of you, and because you are so near, he/she need never stumble or fall. May his/her heart, body, and soul be filled with joy.

17:8 Lord, protect _____ as you would the pupil of your eye. Hide him/her in the shadow of your wings.

18:2 Lord, be a rock, a fortress, and a deliverer to _____ . Help him/her to trust in you as his/her shield, stronghold, and horn of his/her salvation.

18:18-20 Lord, hold _____ steady; lead him/her to a place of safety; reward him/her for doing right and being pure.

18:22-24 May _____ keep close watch on your laws, doing his/her best to keep them all. Then, Lord, give him/her your blessings. You are watching _____'s every step; you know whether he/she is doing what is right and whether or not his/her heart is pure.

18:30 Lord, your way is perfect—always! All your promises are true! Be a shield to _____ as he/she hides in you.

19:7, 8 Lord, your laws are perfect. May _____ find in them protection, wisdom, joy, and light.

19:9, 10 Lord, your laws are pure, eternal, and just. May _____ find them more desirable than gold and sweeter than honey dripping from a honeycomb. Employ your laws to warn and guide him/her away from harm and give him/her success as he/she obeys them.

19:12 Lord, what sins are lurking in the heart of _____ ? Cleanse him/her of these hidden faults. Keep him/her from deliberate wrongs; help him/her to stop doing them.

19:14 May the words of _____'s mouth and the meditations of his/her heart be acceptable and pleasing to you, oh, Lord, our strength and our Redeemer.

143

20:4 O Lord, grant _____ the desire of his/her heart and fulfill all his/her plans and purposes.

20:5 Give to _____ shouts of victory and praise to you for all that you have done.

20:7 May _____'s only boast be in the Lord.

22:22 Enable _____ to praise you to everyone; to stand up before the congregation and testify of the wonderful things you have done.

22:30 (For parents.) May the children of _____ learn to serve you. Help _____ to tell them about the wonders of the Lord.

23:1 Lord, you are _____'s Shepherd. Give to him/her everything he/she needs.

23:2, 3 Enable _____ to lie down and rest in green meadows and lead him/her beside the quiet streams. Restore his/her failing health.

23:4 (For one who is nearing death.) Lord, give _____ victory over fear as he/she approaches the valley of the shadow of death. May he/she realize that you are with him/her, guarding and guiding all the way.

23:6 May your goodness and mercy be with _____ all the days of his/her life and may he/she rejoice in the confidence of living with you forever in your heavenly home.

24:3 Lord, make of _____ a person with clean hands and a pure heart. May he/she flee dishonesty and lying. Your Word promises blessings for all who do this.

25:4, 5 Lord, show _____ the path where he/she should go; point out to him/her the right road in which to walk. Lead him/her; teach him/her. He/she has no hope except in you.

25:6, 7 (For young people.) Forgive the youthful sins of _____ , oh Lord. Look upon him/her through eyes of mercy and forgiveness, through eyes of everlasting love and kindness.

25:8, 9 Lord, you are glad to teach the proper path to all who go astray. You will teach the ways that are right and best to those who humbly turn to you. My prayer is that you do this for _____ .

25:10 May there be full obedience to you on the part of _____ . We know that the path of obedience is fragrant with your lovingkindness and your truth.

25:12 Where, oh Lord, is the man who fears you? May _____ be such a person. We know that you will teach him/her how to choose the best, then he/she will live within your circle of blessing.

25:16, 17 Lord, show _____ your mercy, for he/she is helpless, overwhelmed and in deep distress. His/her problems go from bad to worse. O Lord, save him/her from them all!

25:18, 21 Lord, I pray for _____ that you will see his/her sorrows . . . that you will feel his/her pain and forgive his/her sins. Assign to him/her godliness and integrity as bodyguards.

26:1, 2 Lord, crossexamine _____ to see if he/she has been obedient to your will, trusting you without wavering. Test his/her motives and affections.

26:4, 5 Keep _____ from having fellowship with tricky, two-faced people; they are false and hypocritical. May he/she stay away from the hangouts of sinners.

26:6 May _____ come to you with clean hands, singing a song of thanksgiving and telling about your miracles.

26:11, 12 May _____ walk a straight and narrow path of doing what is right and publicly praise you for keeping him/her from slipping and falling.

27:1 Since you are our light and our salvation, may _____ be emancipated from fear.

27:4 May _____ earnestly seek the privilege of meditating in your temple; living each day of his/her life in your presence and delighting in your incomparable perfections and glory.

27:5, 6 Hide _____ in times of trouble. Set him/her up on a high rock. And may he/she sing your praises with much joy. Be merciful and send him/her the help he/she needs.

27:14 Save _____ from being impatient. May he/she learn to wait on the Lord. Enable him/her to be brave, stouthearted and courageous.

28:7 Lord, you are _____'s strength and his/her shield from every danger. May joy rise in his/her heart until he/she bursts out in songs of praise to you.

30:4, 5 Help _____ to sing to you and give thanks to your holy name, recognizing that weeping may go on all night, but in the morning there is joy.

30:10, 11 Have pity on _____ and help him/her. Turn his/her sorrow into joy. Take away his/her clothes of mourning and give him/her festive garments to rejoice in, so that he/she might sing glad praises to you and keep on thanking you forever!

31:7 May _____ be radiant with joy because of your mercy, because you have listened to his/her troubles and you have seen the crisis in his/her soul.

31:9, 10, 14, 15 (For one deeply afflicted.) O Lord, have mercy on _____ in his/her anguish. His/her eyes are red from weeping; his/her health is broken from sorrow. He/she is pining away with grief.

146

Help him/her to trust you and say, "You alone are my God; my times are in your hands."

32:1 Give to _____ the abundant happiness of those whose guilt has been forgiven; the joy of those whose sins are covered over. Give him/her the relief of those who have confessed their sins and whose records have been cleared by you.

32:5 May _____ admit all his/her sins to you and stop trying to hide them. If he/she will confess them to you, then he/she can have the confidence that you have forgiven him/her and that his/her guilt is all gone.

32:7 Be to _____ a hiding place from every storm of life; keep him/her from getting into trouble. Surround him/her with songs of victory.

32:8 Instruct _____ and teach him/her in the way he/she should go; guide him/her with your eye in every decision he/she needs to make.

32:9 May _____ not be like a senseless horse or mule that has to have a bit in its mouth to keep it in line!

32:10, 11 Your abiding love surrounds those who trust you. So help _____ to rejoice in you and shout for joy.

33:1 Let all the joys of the godly well up in _____ in praise to the Lord, for it is right to praise you.

34:1, 2 May _____ praise you no matter what happens. May he/she constantly speak of your glories and grace and boast of all your kindness to him/her.

34:2, 3 May _____ take heart in the midst of discouragement. May he/she magnify the Lord and exalt your name together with other Christians.

34:4, 5, 7 Free _____ from all his/her fears; may he/she be radiant at what you have done for him/her. May your angel encamp round about _____ and rescue him/her from any and all danger.

34:13, 14 Help _____ to watch his/her tongue and keep his/her lips from lying. May he/she turn from all known sin and spend his/her time in doing good, trying to live in peace with everyone.

34:15, 17 Your eyes, oh Lord, are intently watching all who live good lives; you give attention when we cry to you. Hear _____ when he/she cries to you for help, and save him/her out of all his/her troubles.

34:18-20 Lord, you are close to those whose hearts are breaking; you rescue those who are humbly sorry for their sins. Christians such as _____ do not escape all troubles; he/she has them too. But help him/her in each and every way.

35:28 May _____ tell everyone how great and good you are. May he/she praise you all the day long.

36:5-8 Your steadfast love, Oh Lord, is as great as all the heavens. Your faithfulness reaches beyond the clouds. Your justice is as solid as your mountains. Your decisions are as full of wisdom as the oceans are with water. May _____ take refuge in the shadow of your wings and let him/her drink from your rivers of delight.

37:1, 4 Give _____ victory over envying the wicked. May he/she trust you instead. Help him/her to be kind and good to others. Give him/her the desire of his/her heart.

37:7 Enable _____ to rest in you and wait patiently for you to act. May he/she not be envious of evil men who prosper.

37:8   May _____ stop being angry and turn off all wrath. And may he/she not fret and worry—it only leads to harm.

37:34   Help _____ not to be impatient. May he/she keep traveling steadily along and in due season you will honor him/her with every blessing.

39:1-4   Help _____ to quit complaining, even though the turmoil within him/her grows to the bursting point! Help him/her to realize how brief our time on earth will be. Help him/her to know that he/she is here for but a moment more. Our entire lifetime is but a moment to you.

39:5-7   Lord, we are a proud people, but frail as breath—walking about like a shadow. All our busy rushing ends in nothing. We try to heap up riches for someone else to spend. Our only hope is in you. Help _____ to recognize all this.

40:1-4   Lord, you have lifted _____ out of the pit; you have set his/her feet on a rock and steadied him/her. You have given him/her a new song to sing of praise to our God. May he/she trust you completely and have no confidence in those who are proud.

40:5, 8   O Lord, many a time you have done great miracles for _____ and he/she is ever in your thoughts. Who else can do such glorious things? No one else can be compared with you. So may _____ delight to do your will.

40:9, 10   Empower _____ to tell everyone the Good News that you forgive men's sins. Help him/her not to be timid about it, nor to keep this Good News hidden in his/her heart. May he/she proclaim your lovingkindness and truth to all.

40:16 May the joy of the Lord be given to _____ . May he/she constantly exclaim, "How great God is! Let him be magnified!"

40:17 _____ is poor and needy, yet you are thinking about him/her right now. You are his/her helper and Savior. Come quickly and save him/her out of all his/her troubles. Please don't delay!

42:1 Just as the deer pants for water, may _____ long for you, thirsting for the living God.

43:3, 5 Send out your light and your truth to lead _____ . Why should he/she be so gloomy and discouraged? May he/she trust in you and praise you for your wondrous help.

46:1 Lord, you are our refuge and strength, an ever present help in times of trouble. So enable _____ to overcome fear even though the world blows up and the mountains crumble into the sea.

46:10 Enable _____ to be still and know that you are God.

48:9 Motivate _____ to meditate upon your kindness and your love; and to make your name known throughout the earth.

50:15 Lord, what you want from _____ is true thanks and a fulfillment of promises. You expect him/her to trust you in times of trouble. You will rescue him/her; and may he/she give you the glory.

51:1, 2 O loving God, have mercy on _____ and take away the stain of his/her transgressions. Wash him/her and cleanse him/her of guilt, to be pure again.

51:6 Lord, you deserve and expect that _____ will manifest honesty from the heart; yes, utter sincerity and truthfulness. May such be the case.

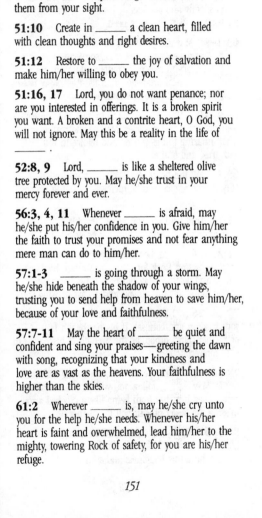

51:7, 9 Sprinkle _____ with the cleansing blood. Wash him/her and he/she shall be whiter than snow. Don't keep looking at his/her sins; erase them from your sight.

51:10 Create in _____ a clean heart, filled with clean thoughts and right desires.

51:12 Restore to _____ the joy of salvation and make him/her willing to obey you.

51:16, 17 Lord, you do not want penance; nor are you interested in offerings. It is a broken spirit you want. A broken and a contrite heart, O God, you will not ignore. May this be a reality in the life of _____ .

52:8, 9 Lord, _____ is like a sheltered olive tree protected by you. May he/she trust in your mercy forever and ever.

56:3, 4, 11 Whenever _____ is afraid, may he/she put his/her confidence in you. Give him/her the faith to trust your promises and not fear anything mere man can do to him/her.

57:1-3 _____ is going through a storm. May he/she hide beneath the shadow of your wings, trusting you to send help from heaven to save him/her, because of your love and faithfulness.

57:7-11 May the heart of _____ be quiet and confident and sing your praises—greeting the dawn with song, recognizing that your kindness and love are as vast as the heavens. Your faithfulness is higher than the skies.

61:2 Wherever _____ is, may he/she cry unto you for the help he/she needs. Whenever his/her heart is faint and overwhelmed, lead him/her to the mighty, towering Rock of safety, for you are his/her refuge.

62:1, 2   Why should _____ be tense with fear when troubles come? O Lord, you are his/her Rock, rescuer, defense, and fortress. So may he/she stand silently and confidently before you, waiting for your solution for every need.

63:1-4   May _____ thirst for you in this parched and weary land. May he/she long to go into your sanctuary to see your strength and glory. Your love and kindness are better than life itself. May he/she praise you and bless you as long as he/she lives.

64:9, 10   May _____ stand in awe and confess your greatness and miracles. May he/she realize what amazing things you do and rejoice in you with trust and praise.

68:1   Fill the heart of _____ with exultation. May he/she rejoice and be merry . . . singing praises to you.

71:1   Lord, you are our refuge. Provide _____ with your protection. Never let him/her be defeated.

71:2, 5, 6   Lord, bend down your ear and be a great protecting Rock for _____ . You are his/her refuge and defense. May he/she put his/her hope in you alone, relying on you and always praising you.

73:24, 26   O Lord, keep on guiding _____ with your wisdom and counsel. If his/her health fails or his/her spirits droop, be the strength of his/her heart . . . forever!

78:36, 57   Many people follow you only with their words. May _____ follow you with his/her whole heart. Keep him/her from being like a crooked arrow, missing the target of your will for his/her life.

84:5, 6   Happy are those who are strong in the Lord; who above all else want to follow your steps. May _____ have this happiness and even though he/she walks through the valley of weeping, may it be a place where pools of blessing and refreshment collect after the rain has fallen.

84:10, 11 One day spent in your Temple is better than a thousand anywhere else. May _____ prefer to be a doorman of the Temple of God than live in palaces of wickedness. Be his/her Light and protector. We know you will not withhold any good thing from _____ if he/she walks uprightly.

85:4-6 O God, revive _____ . Bring him/her back to loving you. Pour out your love and kindness on him/her.

86:11-13 Tell _____ where you want him/her to go and may he/she be ready to go there. May every fiber of his/her being unite in reverence to your name. May he/she praise you with all his/her heart and give glory to your name forever.

92:2 Motivate _____ to rejoice in all your faithfulness. You have done so much for him/her. May he/she be enthused about singing your praises with gladness and joy.

94:19 When doubts fill the mind of _____ ; when his/her heart is in turmoil . . . quiet him/her and give him/her renewed hope and cheer.

95:1, 2 May _____ come before you with a thankful heart . . . singing psalms of praise, giving a joyous shout in honor of the Rock of our salvation.

101:3, 4, 5 Give _____ strength to refuse the low and vulgar things. Help him/her to abhor crooked deals of every kind, to have no part in them; to reject all selfishness and stay away from every evil; to not tolerate secret slandering of his/her neighbors and not permit conceit and pride.

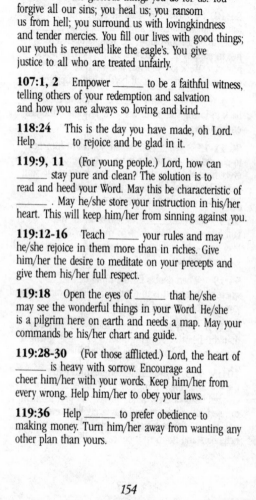

103:1-6 With all his/her heart may _____ bless the holy name of the Lord and not forget all your benefits . . . the glorious things you do for us. You forgive all our sins; you heal us; you ransom us from hell; you surround us with lovingkindness and tender mercies. You fill our lives with good things; our youth is renewed like the eagle's. You give justice to all who are treated unfairly.

107:1, 2 Empower _____ to be a faithful witness, telling others of your redemption and salvation and how you are always so loving and kind.

118:24 This is the day you have made, oh Lord. Help _____ to rejoice and be glad in it.

119:9, 11 (For young people.) Lord, how can _____ stay pure and clean? The solution is to read and heed your Word. May this be characteristic of _____ . May he/she store your instruction in his/her heart. This will keep him/her from sinning against you.

119:12-16 Teach _____ your rules and may he/she rejoice in them more than in riches. Give him/her the desire to meditate on your precepts and give them his/her full respect.

119:18 Open the eyes of _____ that he/she may see the wonderful things in your Word. He/she is a pilgrim here on earth and needs a map. May your commands be his/her chart and guide.

119:28-30 (For those afflicted.) Lord, the heart of _____ is heavy with sorrow. Encourage and cheer him/her with your words. Keep him/her from every wrong. Help him/her to obey your laws.

119:36 Help _____ to prefer obedience to making money. Turn him/her away from wanting any other plan than yours.

119:61   Evil people will try to drag _____ into sin, but may he/she be firmly anchored in your laws.

119:71, 72   Your punishment, Lord, is often the best thing that can happen to us. May _____ respond to your chastening by paying attention to your laws. Those laws are more valuable than millions in silver and gold.

119:97-100   _____ can be wiser than his/her enemies and even wiser than his/her teachers . . . if he/she meditates on your law and your testimonies. Encourage him/her to do this.

119:105   Lord, keep _____ from stumbling. Use your Word as a flashlight to light his/her path and may he/she always obey your wonderful laws.

119:125   Give _____ common sense to apply your rules to everything he/she does.

139:1-3   Lord, you have examined _____'s heart and you know everything about him/her. You know when he/she is sitting or standing. I pray you will chart the path ahead for him/her and tell him/her where to rest . . . when to stop and when to go.

139:23   Search _____ and know his/her heart. Test him/her and point out any wicked way in his/her life, and lead him/her in the path that is everlasting.

141:3, 4   Help _____ to keep his/her mouth shut and his/her lips sealed. Take away his/her lust for evil things. May he/she not want to be with sinners, doing what they do.

145:5-7   Teach _____ to meditate about your glory, splendor, majesty, and miracles. May your awe-inspiring deeds be on his/her tongue, proclaiming your greatness.

Assurance   Psa. 36:5-8; 40:1-4; 56:3, 4, 11; Rom. 8:35, 38, 39; Heb. 10:22; 1 John 4:17; 5:13, 14.

Backsliding (see Perseverance)   Psa. 85:4-6; Matt. 24:12; Luke 8:13; 15:11-24; Gal. 5:7; 2 Tim. 3:13; Heb. 2:1.

Bible (Word of God)   Psa. 1:2; 18:22-24; 19:7-10; 119:9-16, 18, 105; Matt. 4:4; Luke 4:4-13; 11:28; 24:45; John 5:39; 17:15, 17; Acts 17:11; 19:20; 1 Thess. 5:20; 2 Tim. 2:15; 3:16; Heb. 4:12.

Chastening   Psa. 119:71, 72; John 15:2; Heb. 12:5, 6, 10.

Children   Psa. 22:30; Matt. 18:3, 4, 6; Luke 18:16; 1 Cor. 13:11; Eph. 6:1; Col. 3:20.

Christian Conduct   Psa. 26:1, 2, 11, 12; Rom. 13:13; 1 Cor. 3:3, 13; 4:19, 20; 6:13, 18; 10:31; Gal. 4:6, 7; 5:20; Eph. 4:1, 2; Phil. 1:27; 4:8; Col. 1:10; 3:10; 1 Tim. 4:12; 6:11; 2 Tim. 2:22; Heb. 4:13; 1 John 2:6.

Church Attendance   Psa. 27:4; 63:1, 4; 84:10, 11; Luke 4:16; 24:53; Acts 2:42, 46; Heb. 10:25.

Cleansing (see Purity)   Psa. 19:12; 24:3; 51:7, 9, 10; 119:9; Luke 11:39; 1 Thess. 5:23; 2 Tim. 2:21; James 4:8; 1 John 1:9; 2:1, 2.

Compassion (see Love)   Matt. 25:34-36; Luke 10:33-37; 14:13; Acts 9:36; Rom. 12:13, 15; Col. 3:12; 1 Pet. 3:8.

Complaining (Murmuring)   Psa. 39:1-4; 1 Cor. 10:10; Phil. 2:14; Heb. 3:7, 8; James 5:9; Jude 16-19.

Consecration (Commitment)   Matt. 19:29; 22:37, 38; Luke 5:27, 28; 18:28-30; 19:17; John 12:3; Acts 20:24; Rom. 12:1; 1 Cor. 9:25; Phil. 3:8; Col. 3:17; 1 Thess. 1:9.

Contentment   Psa. 23:2, 3; 37:7; 46:10; Phil. 4:11, 12; 1 Tim. 6:6; Heb. 13:5.

Discipleship   Matt. 10:38; 16:24; Luke 9:23; 14:26, 33; John 8:31; 12:25, 26.

Faith   Psa. 56:3, 4; 62:1, 2; Matt. 8:26; 14:27; 21:21, 22; Acts 6:8; 11:24; Rom. 4:20; Eph. 6:13; Col. 2:7; Heb. 11:6, 8; 1 Pet. 1:7; 2 Pet. 1:5-7; 1 John 5:4.

Faithfulness Psa. 36:5-8; Matt. 24:42, 44; 25:20, 21; Luke 16:10; Acts 11:23; 1 Cor. 4:2; 15:58; 16:2; 1 John 2:17.

Family Psa. 22:30; Eph. 6:1, 4; Col. 3:20, 21.

Fear Psa. 27:1; 34:4-7; 46:1; 56:3, 4, 11; 62:1, 2; Matt. 8:26; 14:27; 28:10; Luke 12:32; John 14:1; Rom. 10:9-11; 2 Tim. 1:7; 1 John 4:18.

Fellowship Psa. 1:1; 26:4, 5; 34:2, 3; 119:61; Gal. 6:2, 10; Eph. 1:15, 16; 4:16; 5:7; 1 John 1:7.

Food Matt. 6:25, 28, 31; 25:34-36; Luke 10:42; 12:22, 23, 29-31; John 6:27.

Forgiveness Psa. 32:1; 51:1, 2, 7, 9; Matt. 6:11-13; 18:21, 22; Luke 6:31; 17:3, 4; Col. 3:13; 1 John 1:9.

Freedom John 8:32, 34-36; Rom. 6:22; Eph. 5:13; 1 Pet. 2:16.

Fruit-bearing (see Soul-winning; Witnessing) Psa. 107:1, 2; Matt. 13:23; Luke 6:43-45; 13:6, 7; John 15:2, 5, 8.

God's Care Psa. 23:1; 25:16, 17; Matt. 10:30, 31; Luke 12:6, 7, 28; Acts 2:25; 18:9, 10; Rom. 8:28, 31.

Gratitude (Thankfulness) Psa. 7:17; 26:6; 103:1-6; Luke 17:15, 16; John 11:41; Eph. 1:15, 16; 5:19, 20.

Greatness Psa. 35:28; Matt. 18:3, 4; 20:26, 27; 23:11, 12; Luke 9:46-48.

Growth (Spiritual) 1 Cor. 3:2; Eph. 4:13, 14; Heb. 6:1; 1 Pet. 2:2; 2 Pet. 3:18.

Guidance (Instruction) Psa. 25:4, 5; 32:8; 43:3; 73:24, 26; 86:11, 13; 139:1-3; John 10:4, 5, 27; 2 Tim. 3:16.

Holiness Psa. 34:13, 14; Rom. 12:1; 1 Cor. 3:16, 17; 15:34; Eph. 1:4; 4:19, 24; 2 Tim. 1:9; 1 Pet. 1:15; 2 Pet. 3:11, 13.

Holy Spirit Luke 1:37; 12:12; Acts 1:8; 2:17; 4:8-12, 31; 6:3; 9:31; 10:45; 11:24; 13:52; 16:6, 7; Rom. 8:4-6, 9-14, 27; 15:13; 1 Cor. 2:9, 10; Gal. 5:17, 22, 23; Eph. 3:16; 4:30; 5:18; 1 Thess. 5:19; 1 John 2:27;.

Honesty (Truthfulness) Psa. 51:6; Luke 16:10; Rom. 12:17; 13:13; Eph. 4:25; Phil. 4:8.

Humility Matt. 5:3, 5, 7; 18:3, 4; Luke 9:46-48; 14:11; 18:9, 14; 22:26; John 7:18; 12:43; 13:14, 15; Rom. 11:20, 22; 12:3, 10, 16; 1 Cor. 10:12; Eph. 4:2; 1 Pet. 5:5.

Joy Psa. 16:8, 9; 28:7; 30:10; 31:7; 40:16; 51:12; John 15:11; 16:24; Acts 2:26; 13:52; 23:11; 27:25; Rom. 15:13; Col. 1:11; 1 Pet. 1:8; 1 John 1:4.

Judging (Judgment) Matt. 7:1; Luke 6:41, 42; Rom. 14:1-5, 10, 13; 1 Cor. 3:13; 4:4, 5; Gal. 6:1.

Love Matt. 10:37; 22:37, 38; John 13:34, 35; 14:15, 21; 15:17; 21:17; Rom. 8:35, 38, 39; 12:10; 13:9, 10; 1 Cor. 12:31; 1 Cor. 13; Eph. 3:17, 18; Phil. 2:2; James 4:11; 1 Pet. 3:8; 4:8.

Marriage 1 Cor. 7:1-3, 8, 37, 38; 13:7; Eph. 5:22, 25; Col. 3:18, 19; Titus 2:5; 1 Pet. 3:1-7.

Material Needs Matt. 6:11, 33; Acts 9:36; 1 John 3:17.

Missions (see Witnessing; Soul-winning) Matt. 28:19; Luke 10:2; Acts 13:48, 49; 16:6, 7; 17:6, 7; 20:24; Rom. 1:14-16.

Money (Treasures; Stewardship) Psa. 119:36; Matt. 6:18, 19; Luke 6:38; 8:3; 12:21, 33; 16:13; 18:22; 21:2-4; Acts 2:45; 20:35; 1 Cor. 9:11-14; 16:2; Phil. 4:18, 19; 1 Tim. 6:6, 10, 18, 19; 2 Tim. 3:2; Heb. 13:5.

Music (Singing) Psa. 7:17; 9:1, 2; 13:5, 6; 26:6; 28:7; 30:10; 57:7; 92:2; 95:1, 2; 1 Cor. 14:15; Eph. 5:19, 20; Col. 3:16.

Obedience Psa. 1:2; 25:10; 26:1, 2; 32:9; 119:36; Matt. 19:17-19; 21:6; Luke 6:46-49; 20:25; John 9:7; 10:4, 5, 27; 14:15, 21, 24; Acts 5:29; 9:6; 16:6, 7; 1 Cor. 4:2; 9:16; Titus 3:1; 1 Pet. 1:14; 1 John 2:5; 3:24; 5:3.

Patience Psa. 27:14; 37:7, 34; 39:1-4; 46:10; Rom. 12:12; 1 Cor. 14:4; Eph. 4:2; Col. 3:12; Heb. 12:1; James 1:4, 19; 2 Pet. 3:8, 9.

Peace John 14:27; 16:33; 20:26, 27; Rom. 12:18; 14:19; 15:13; Rom. 15:13; Col. 3:15; 1 Pet. 3:11.

Perseverance (Dependability; Constancy) Psa. 37:34; Matt. 24:12, Luke 8:15; Acts 18:9, 10; 20:24; 1 Cor. 16:8, 9, 13; Gal. 1:6; 6:9; Phil. 3:13, 14; Col. 1:11, 23; 1 Thess. 3:2, 3; 2 Tim. 1:9; Heb. 3:6, 14; 10:36; 12:1, 3.

Power Luke 24:49; Acts 1:8; 4:8-12; 6:8; Rom. 8:37; 9:17; Eph. 3:16; Phil. 4:13; 2 Tim. 1:7; Heb. 4:12.

Praise (See Rejoicing) Psa. 9:1, 2; 22:22; 34:1, 2; 57:7; 63:1-4; 64:9, 10; 71:2, 5, 6; 86:11-13; 92:2; 95:1, 2; 103:1-6; 118:24; 145:5-7; Luke 1:46, 47, 49, 64; 2:20; 19:37; Rom. 15:11; Acts 2:26; Eph. 1:12; Heb. 13:15; Jude 24, 25.

Prayer (Petition) Psa. 5:5; Matt. 7:7; 21:21, 22; 26:41; John 11:41; 14:13, 14; 16:23, 24; 1 Cor. 14:15; Eph. 3:12; 6:18; Phil. 4:6, 7; Col. 4:2; 1 Tim. 2:1, 2; Heb. 4:16; 10:22; 1 Pet. 4:7; 1 John 5:14; Jude 20.

Pride Psa. 20:7; Luke 18:9, 14; John 12:13; Rom. 11:20, 22; 12:16; 14:1-5; 1 Cor. 4:7, 8; 8:1, 2; 13:4; Gal. 5:26; 6:3, 10; 1 Tim. 6:17; 2 Tim. 3:2.

Protection Psa. 5:11; 17:8; 27:5, 6; 28:7; 32:7; 36:5-8; 57:1-3; 61:2; 62:1, 2; 71:2, 5, 6; Col. 2:4.

Purity Psa. 24:3; 51:1, 2, 7, 9, 10; 119:9, 11; Matt. 5:8, 9, 13; Luke 11:34-36; Phil. 2:15, 16; 4:8; 1 Thess. 4:3, 4, 7; 1 Tim. 1:5; 2 Tim. 2:22; James 3:17; 1 Pet. 1:22; 1 John 3:1-3.

Rejoicing (Thankfulness; Gratitude) Psa. 5:11; 20:5; 92:2; 95:1, 2; 118:24; Luke 15:7; Acts 13:48; Rom. 12:12, 15; Phil. 1:26; 4:4; 1 Thess. 5:16, 18.

Revival Psa. 51:12; 139:23; Rom. 13:11, 12.

Rewards (Judgment Day)   Matt. 24:42, 44; 25:20, 21;
    Luke 6:20-22, 27, 35; 18:28-30; 19:17; Rom. 2:7, 16;
    Phil. 3:14; Heb. 11:26.
Satan (Devil)   Matt. 4:4, 10; Luke 4:4-13; Eph. 6:11, 16;
    2 Tim. 2:26; James 4:7; 1 Pet. 5:8, 9.
Second Coming   Matt. 24:42, 44; Luke 12:35-40; 21:28, 34,
    36; 1 Cor. 4:4, 5; 1 Thess. 1:3, 10; 5:5, 6; 2 Tim. 4:8;
    Titus 2:13; James 5:7, 8; 1 Pet. 1:13; 2 Pet. 3:11-14;
    1 John 2:28; 3:1-3.
Sin   Psa. 19:12; 32:5; 119:61; 139:23; Gal. 5:21; Eph. 4:19,
    24; 5:3; Col. 3:5, 9; 1 Thess. 5:22; 2 Tim. 2:21, 22;
    Titus 2:14; James 1:21; 1 Pet. 2:11; 2 Pet. 2:10; 1 John 2:1,
    2, 16; 1 John 3:6, 9; Jude 23.
Sincerity   Psa. 78:36, 57; Matt. 23:18; Rom. 12:17; Phil. 1:10;
    Titus 2:7.
Soul-winning (see Fruit-bearing; Missions)   Matt. 4:19;
    22:9, 10; 28:10, 19; Luke 5:4; 10:2; 15:4-7; John 4:35-38;
    Rom. 1:14-16; 9:2, 3; 1 Cor. 9:19-22.
Spiritual Strength   Psa. 101:3; 1 Cor. 16:13; Eph. 3:16;
    6:10, 16; Col. 2:7; 2 Tim. 2:1,-3; 4:7; 1 John 5:4.
Temptation   Matt. 4:4; 26:41; Luke 4:4-13; 8:13; 1 Cor.
    10:13; Heb. 2:18; 12:1, 16; James 4:7; 1 Pet. 2:11.
Tongues (Speech)   Psa. 19:14; 34:13, 14; 141:3, 4; 145:5, 7;
    Matt. 12:36, 37; 15:8; Luke 1:64; Rom. 10:9-11; Eph. 4:29;
    5:4; 1 Tim. 1:6; 2 Tim. 2:16, 23; Titus 2:8; James 5:9;
    1 Pet. 3:10; 2 Pet. 2:18.
Trials (Afflictions; Burdens; Suffering)   Psa. 9:9, 10; 31:9-15;
    34:18-20; 119:28-30; Matt. 13:21; Luke 6:22; Rom. 5:3-5;
    8:18, 28; Phil. 1:29; James 1:2, 3; 1 Pet. 3:17; 4:12, 13.
Trust (see Assurance; Faith)   Psa. 13:5, 6; 18:2; 40:1-4; 50:13;
    56:3, 4, 11; 57:1-3; 61:2; Matt. 6:34; 1 Tim. 6:17; 2 Tim. 1:12.
Unity (Oneness)   Rom. 15:5; 1 Cor. 1:10; 12:12-27; Eph. 4:16;
    Phil. 1:27.
Unsaved   John 5:24; Acts 2:38; 3:19; Rom. 1:14-16; 9:2, 3;
    10:1; Heb. 2:3; 3:15.
Unselfishness   Rom. 15:1; 1 Cor. 10:24, 32, 33; 12:25; 13:5;
    Phil. 2:3-7; 4:5; 1 Pet. 4:10.
Victory   Psa. 20:5; Matt. 4:4; Rom. 8:31, 37; 1 Cor. 3:3;
    1 John 5:4.
Vindictiveness   Rom. 12:17, 19; 1 Thess. 5:15; 1 Pet. 3:9.
Wisdom   Psa. 119:97-100; Acts 6:3; 1 Cor. 1:19, 20; 2:15;
    3:18, 19; Eph. 1:17; 4:13, 18; Col. 1:9; 3:16; 2 Tim. 3:14, 15;
    James 3:17.
Witnessing (see Fruit-bearing; Missions; Soul-winning)   Psa.
    40:9, 10; 48:9; 107:1, 2; Luke 1:79; 8:16, 39; 9:26; 12:8;
    24:48; John 15:2, 5, 8; Acts 4:20; 5:28; 8:4; 13:48, 49;
    20:24; 22:15; 26:16, 18; Rom. 1:14-16; 10:9-11; 1 Cor. 1:5;
    Phil. 1:20; 2:15, 16; Col. 1:28; 4:5; 2 Tim. 1:8; 4:2; Jude 23.

Worldliness Psa. 1:1; 26:4, 5; Rom. 12:2; Gal. 5:21; 6:14;
Col. 3:1, 2; 1 John 2:15.

Worry Psa. 23:2, 3; 37:8; Matt. 6:25, 34; John 14:1;
Phil. 4:6; 1 Pet. 5:7.

Worship (see Praise) Psa. 5:7; 16:5; 57:7; 64:9, 10; Luke
1:46, 47, 49; 5:26; 19:37; John 1:21-24; 4:21-24; Rom. 12:1;
Eph. 5:19; 1 Tim. 1:17; Heb. 12:28.

Yieldedness Matt. 19:29; Rom. 6:13, 16, 18, 19; 9:21.

Youth Psa. 25:6, 7; 103:5; 119:9, 11; 1 Tim. 4:12; 2 Tim.
2:22; 1 Pet. 5:5.

Zeal Acts 17:6, 7; 18:24, 25; Rom. 12:11; Titus 2:14; Jude 3.

Tear Out This Form
and Mail Today
SPECIAL PRICE

As you enjoy this treasury of prayers from God's Word, you'll probably think of others—friends and loved ones—whose lives would be enriched by this booklet.

If so, take a moment right now to order extra copies for gifts. The regular price is $2.95 each. Your special price from GRASON is 4 copies for $8.00 ($2.00 each) plus $.75 postage and handling. Any additional copies (more than 4) will cost you only $1.50 each.

☐ YES, please send me 4 copies of POCKET PRAYERS at the special price of $8.00 plus $.75 postage and handling (regularly priced at $2.95).

_____Additional copies for $1.50 each.

_____

Name

_____

Address

_____

City   State   Zip

Send this order form and your payment today to:

A ministry of the Billy Graham Association

Box 1240, Minneapolis, MN 55440
(612)333-0725   XQ